Adolf Loos

Villa Muller

1930
Prague

アドルフ・ロース
ミュラー邸
1930　プラハ

Banana Books

書斎暖炉のタイル　*Fireplace Tiles in the Library*

ミュラー邸

Villa Muller

Photos: Kazuyoshi Miyamoto　Text: Takeshi Goto

目　次

- ◇住宅写真　　　　　　　　　　　　　　　4-9,14-33
- ◇図面　　　　　　　　　　　　　　　　　10-13,34-37
- ◇アドルフ・ロースの現代性
  - 装飾はいらない：生活の多様性へ　　　　38
  - 平面図はいらない：ラウムプランへ　　　40
  - 統一性はいらない：ミュラー邸へ　　　　44
  - 高価な素材はいらない：着衣のような建築へ　48
  - 想像力はいらない：ファンタジーをこえて　54

Contents

- ◇Photos of the Villa Muller　　　　　　4-9,14-33
- ◇Drawings　　　　　　　　　　　　　　10-13,34-37
- ◇Modernity of Adolf Loos
  - Ornament is Unnecessary: toward a Variety of Life　39
  - Plans are Unnecessary: toward Raumplan　41
  - Uniformity is Unnecessary: toward the Villa Muller　45
  - Expensive Material is Unnecessary:
    toward Architecture like Clothes　49
  - Imagination is Unnecessary: beyond Fantasy　55

敷地は南西から北東に向けて傾斜した小高い丘の上にあって、北東方向にプラハの市街を見渡すことができる。南側の前面道路から門扉をくぐり、左に折れて玄関にアプローチする。車はそのまま玄関を通り過ぎて西側へまわり、スロープをおりて一層分下のガレージへと収容される。東側には庭園がひろがっている。

The site is on a hill sloping down toward the northeast. If you look to the northeast, you can see all of Prague. To approach the entrance, go through the gate from the front street in the southwest of the site and then turn left. Cars pass by the entrance towards the west to the parking space at the bottom of the slope, just under the house. There is a garden on the east side.

▲ 南東ファサード
キュービックなヴォリュームを突出させたり欠き取ったりする操作が特徴的である。四階のダイニング・ルームが内側から押し出されて突出している。そのヴォリュームを庇がわりに使って、ベンチが置かれているのが見える。

Southeast Façade
Worthy of note is the detailed control of shapes, such as the increasing or lessening of cubic dimension. The dining room is projected off of the 4th floor and the projections act as eaves, with a bench underneath.

北東ファサード
斜面の下から北東ファサードを見上げる。三階のメイン・ホールと五階の主寝室が北東に面していて、プラハの市街を見下ろしている。斜面を利用してメイン・ホールにテラスのヴォリュームが、西側には車寄せのヴォリュームが寄り添って、群造形をつくりだしている。

Northeast Façade
Looking up to the northeast façade from the bottom of the slope, Prague city can be seen from the main hall on the 3rd floor and the main bedroom on the 5th floor. The total area of the building takes advantage of the slope; the relation between the main hall and the terrace, and the porch set upon the western side.

南西ファサード
玄関側のファサード。左右対称を基本にして立面が構成されているが、微妙に均衡をずらしている。さまざまな窓の配列パターンのスタディが残っている。

Southwest Façade
Entrance façade. The elevation is basically symmetric with a slight displacement. There remains a study with various window alignment patterns.

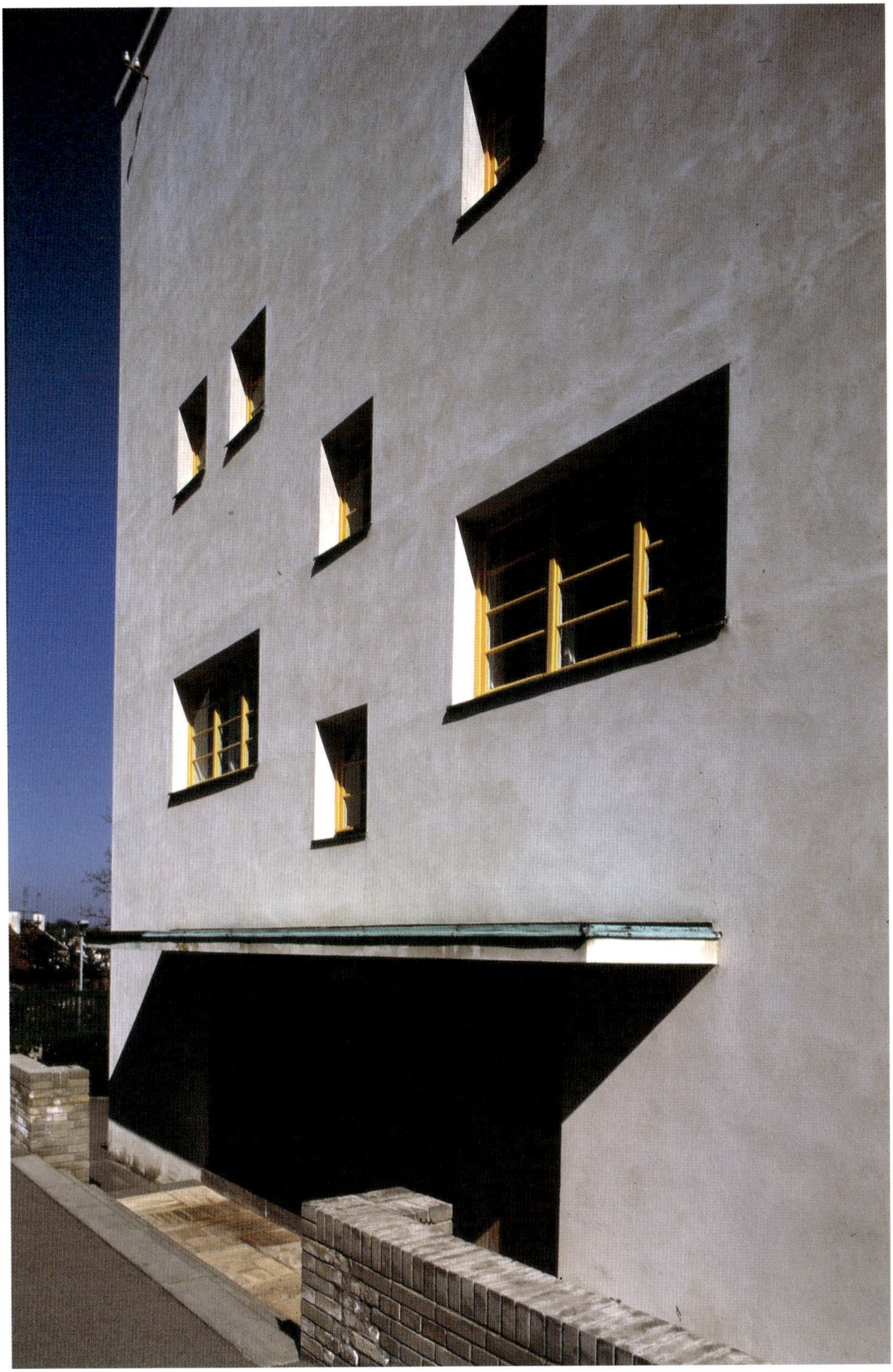

▲ 少し奥まったところに、この住宅の規模としてはとても慎ましい玄関扉がある。

The entrance door, which is located in a remote place, is very small for a house of this scale.

車を廻して来るまでのあいだ待機するベンチを中心に配して、左右対称の構成になっている。左側が玄関扉である。右側には倉庫の窓が開けられている。壁面は大理石のトラバーチンで仕上げられている。トラバーチンは巴形のパターンで貼られているが、これはこの住宅の空間構成の原理を示しているようにも見える。

The entrance door is symmetrically organized with the bench in the center, where one could wait for a car. On the left side is the entrance door and on the right side, a storage window. The walls are finished with marble travertine. Travertine has a tornado pattern and this might express the principles of spatial compositions within this residence.

Floor plans

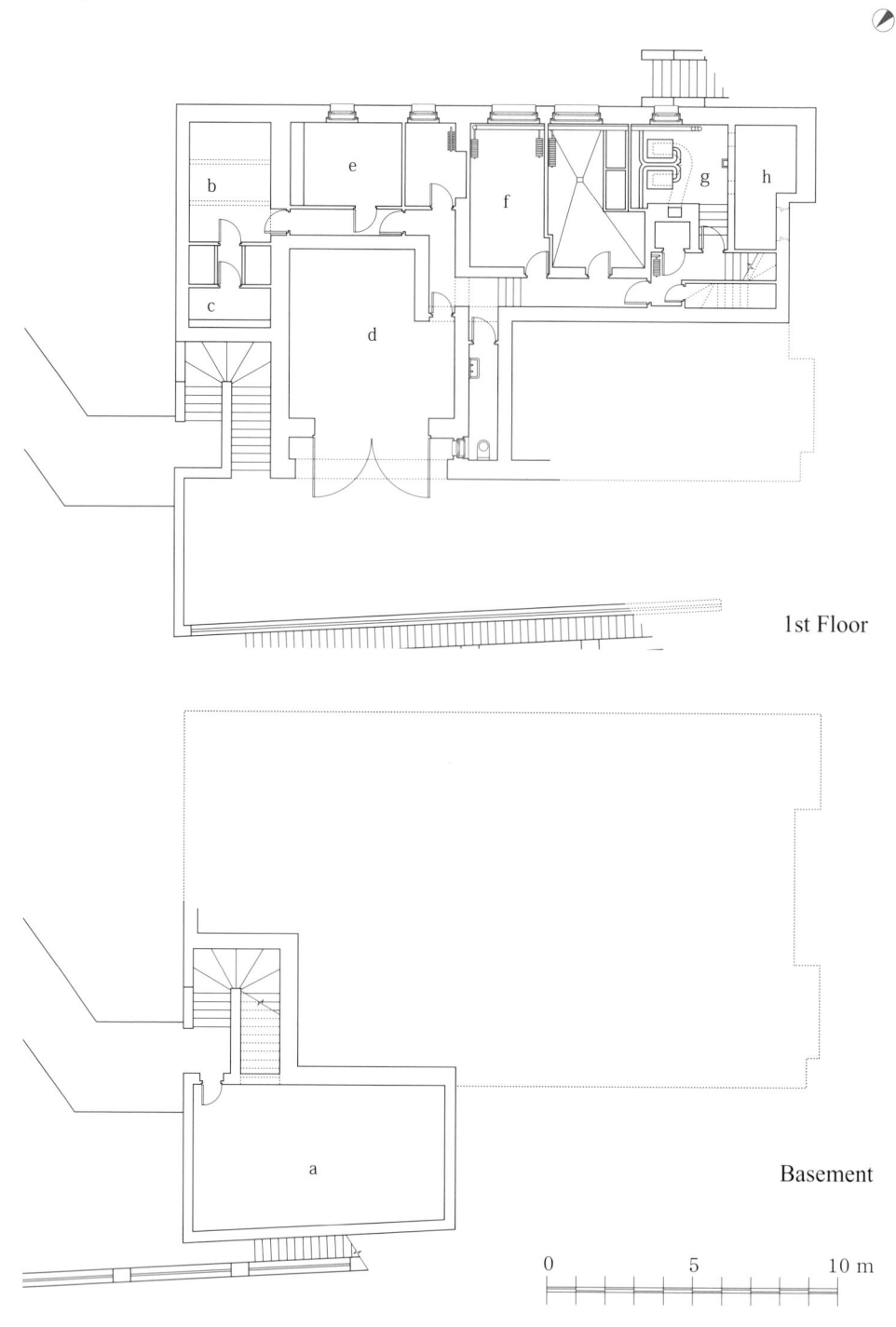

1st Floor

Basement

0   5   10 m

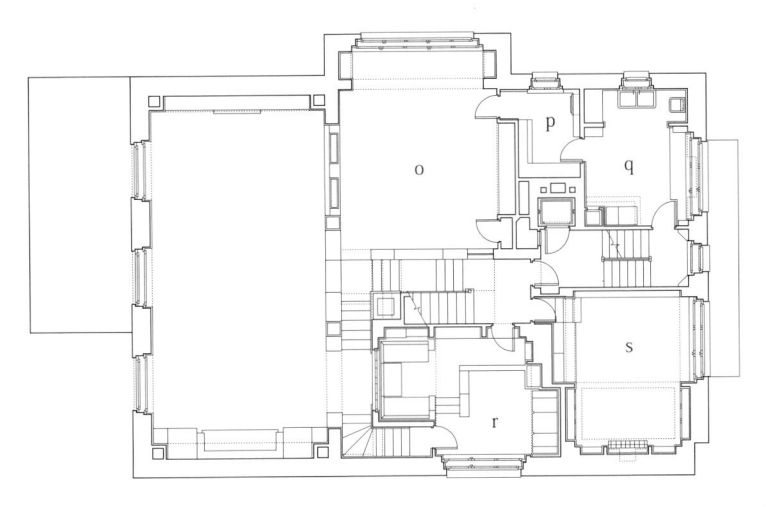

3rd Floor

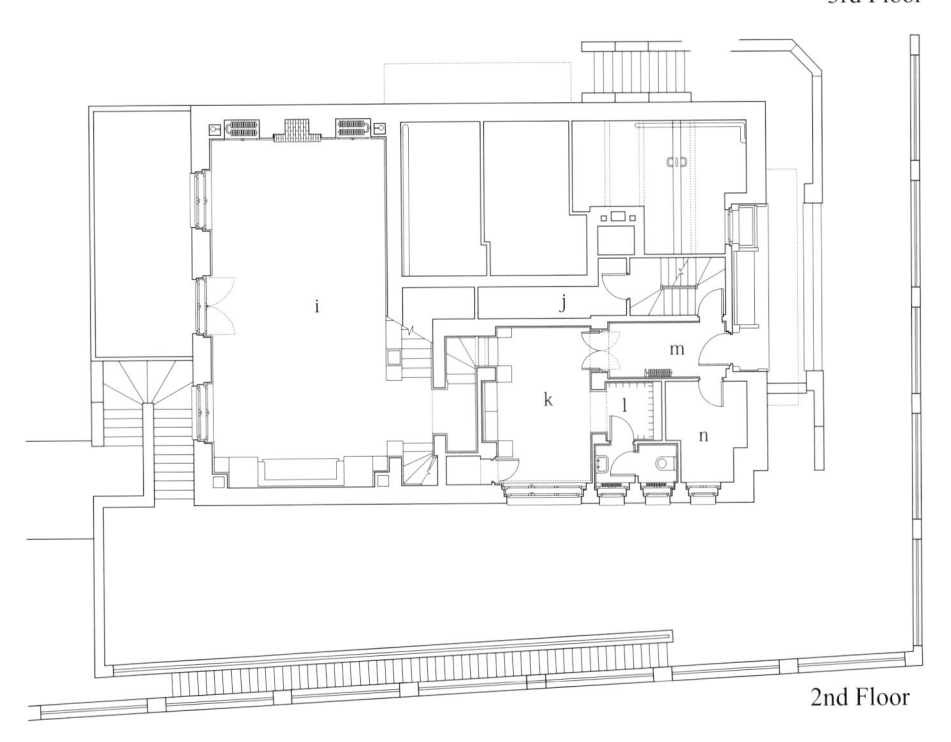

2nd Floor

a.倉庫 b.倉庫 c.ワインセラー d.車庫 e.使用人室 f.洗濯室 g.ボイラー室 h.石炭倉庫 i.メイン・ホール j.食品庫 k.前室 l.クローク m.エントランス n.談話室 o.ダイニング・ルーム p.前室 q.キッチン r.婦人室 s.書斎

a.Storage b.Storage c.Cellar d.Garage e.Servants' room f.Laundry room g.Boiler room h.Coal storage i.Main Hall j.Provisions store k.Front chamber l.Cloakroom m.Entrance n.Conversation room o.Dining room p.Front chamber q.Kitchen r.Boudoir s.Library

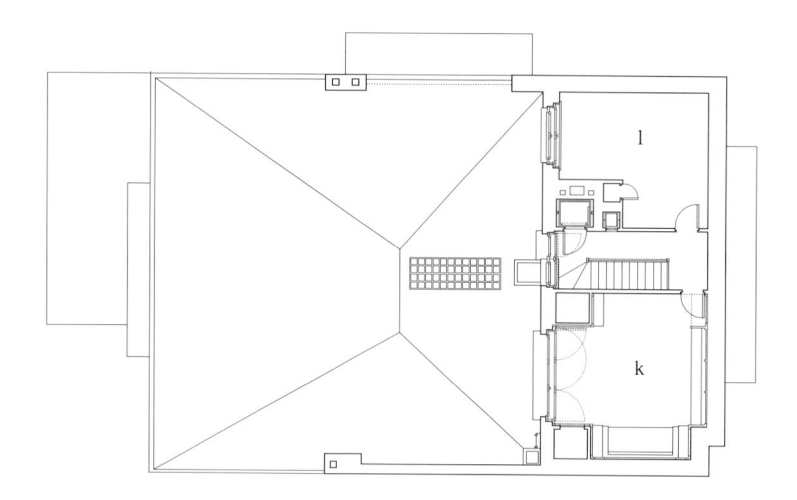

5th Floor

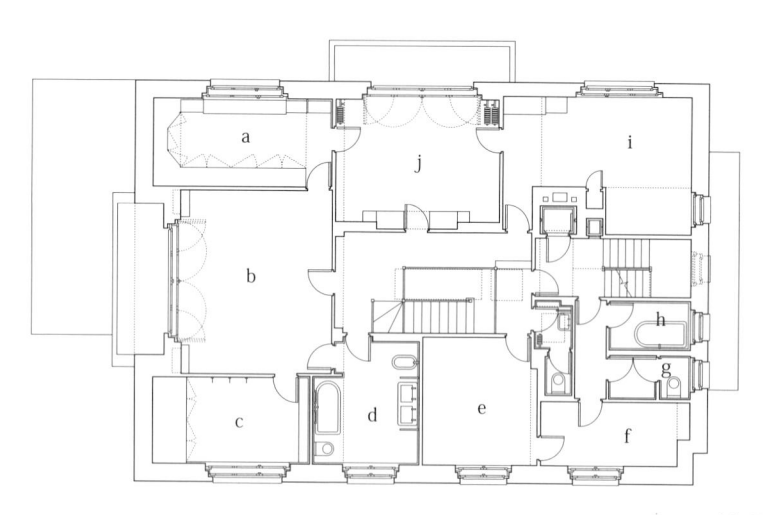

4th Floor

0   5   10 m

a.婦人用クローゼット　b.主寝室　c.紳士用クローゼット　d.バス・ルーム　e.ゲスト・ルーム　f.使用人室
g.トイレ　h.バス・ルーム　i.プレイ・ルーム　j.子供室　k.サマー・ブレックファスト・ルーム　l.屋根裏部屋

a.Lady's dressing room b.Main bedroom c.Gentleman's dressing room d.Bathroom e.Guest room
f.Servants' room g.W.C h.Bathroom i.Playroom j.Children's room k.Summer breakfast room l.Attic room

Axonometric Perspective

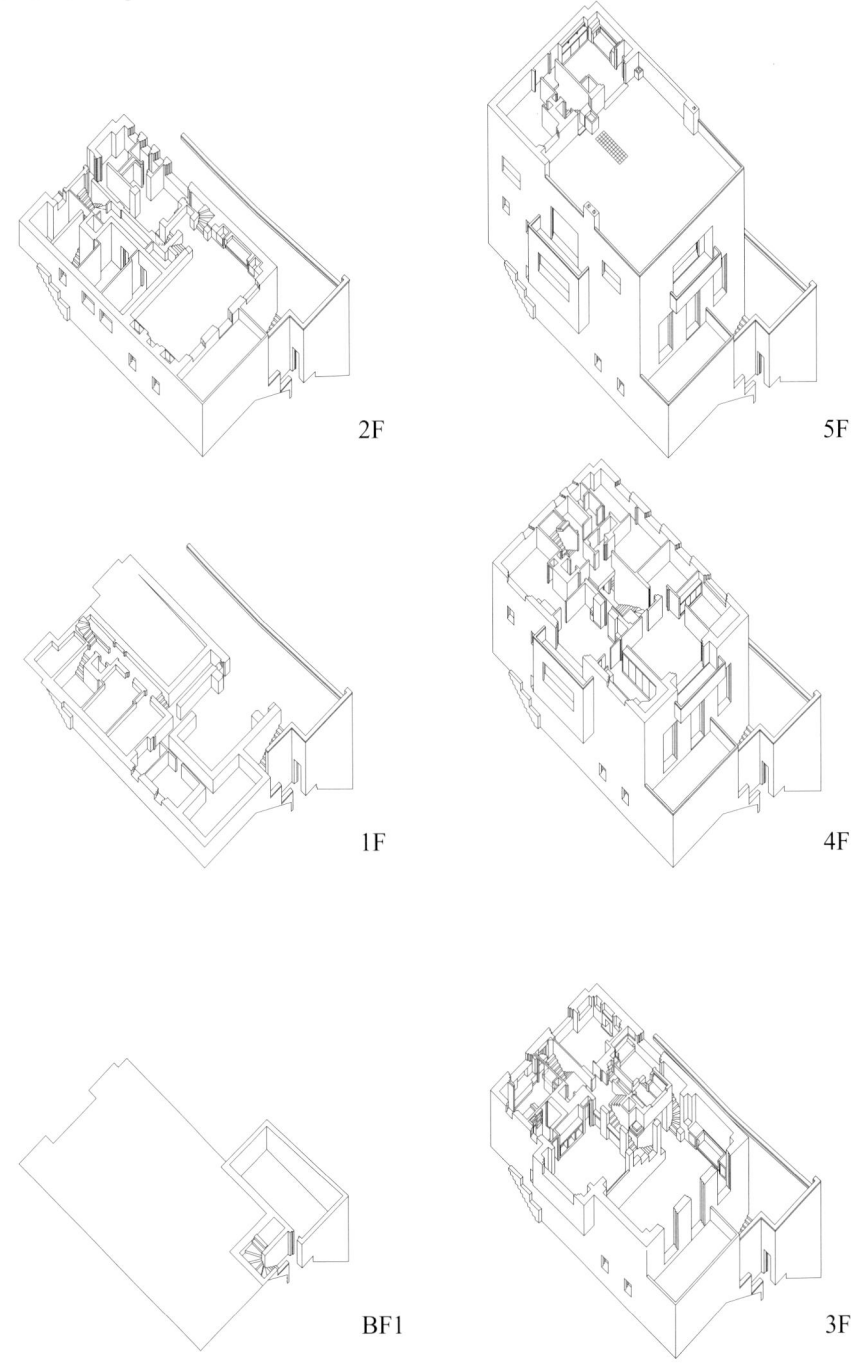

2F

5F

1F

4F

BF1

3F

13

▶ 玄関に続く前室。ここでも玄関と同じように左右対称の構成が取られている。クローク・ルームが併設されているので、コートや荷物を預けて一休みできるように、中央にベンチが設えられている。

Front chamber to the entrance. The room is symmetrically organized similar to the entrance. A cloakroom is present, and there is a bench in the center near the cloakroom.

▶ メイン・ホールからダイニング・ルーム、寝室へと上がっていく階段が見える。彫像の上には、寝室への階段の裏側が見えている。右上には婦人室の窓。空間が立体的に組み合わさっているのがよくわかる。

Stairway from the main hall up to the dining room and the bedrooms. You can see the backside of the stairway to the bedrooms which are above a sculpture. The boudoir window is above and to the right. It is obvious that these spaces are sterically composed.

▲ 大理石のチポリーノで仕上げられた二層分の天井高があるメイン・ホール。奥には、少しレベルがあがってダイニング・ルームが見える。チポリーノの壁には水槽が二つ埋め込んであって、ダイニング・ルームからの光を透過している。壁に掛けられた絵画の二次元世界と、大理石の壁に埋め込まれた水槽のガラス面がとてもよく似ている。暖炉や照明器具も左右対称に設けられているのがわかる。左手にはテラスがあり、二つの窓とテラス扉がやはり左右対称にある。

The main hall, with a height of two floors, is finished with marble cipollino. You can see the dining room with a higher level at the back. There are two aquariums installed in the cipollino wall and they allow light to penetrate from the dining room to the hall. The two dimensional world created by the pictures on the wall and the glass surfaces of the aquariums complement each other. The fireplace and lighting equipment are symmetrically set. There is a terrace to the left and two windows, as well as the terrace door. All are set up symmetrically as well.

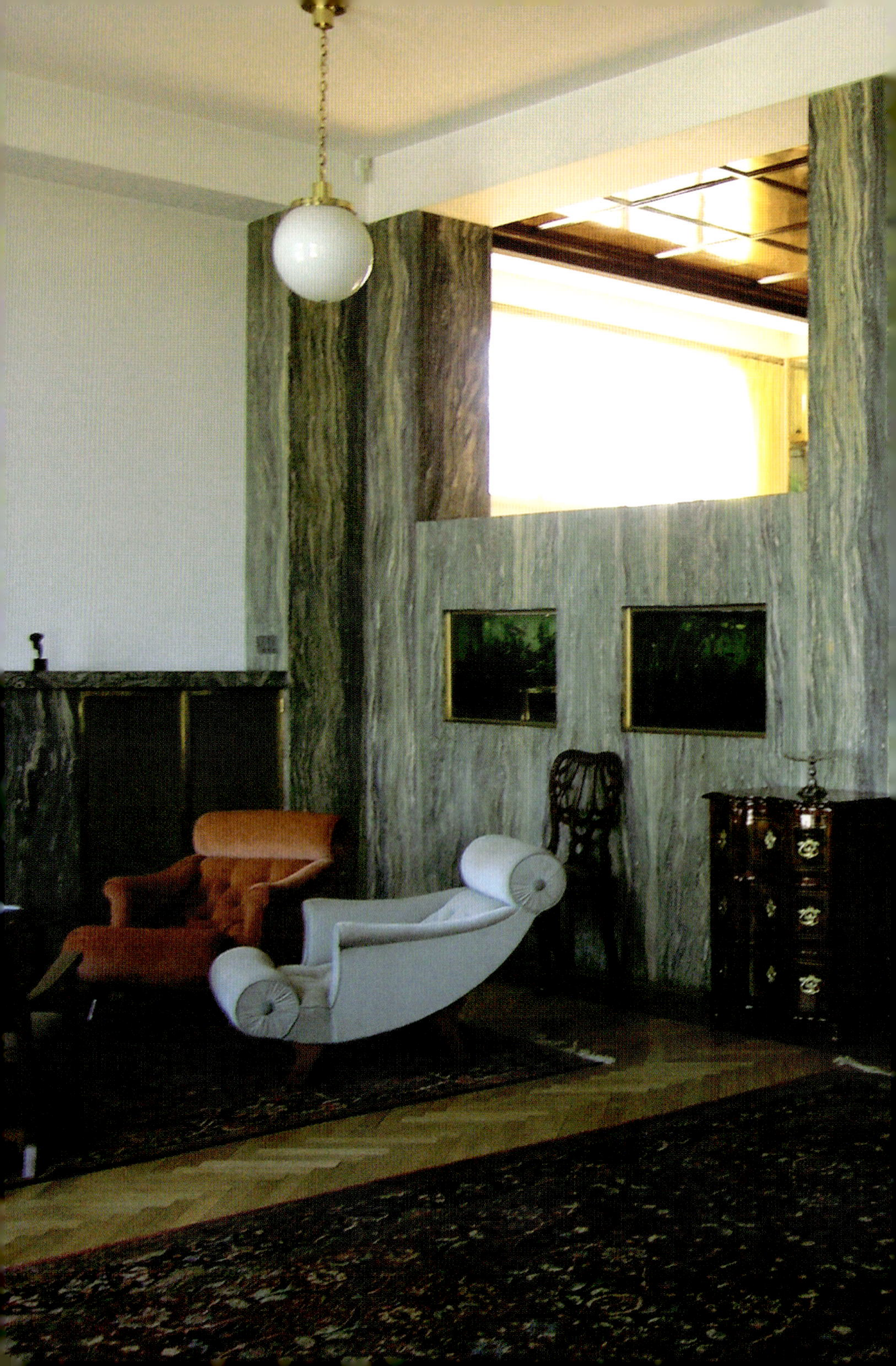

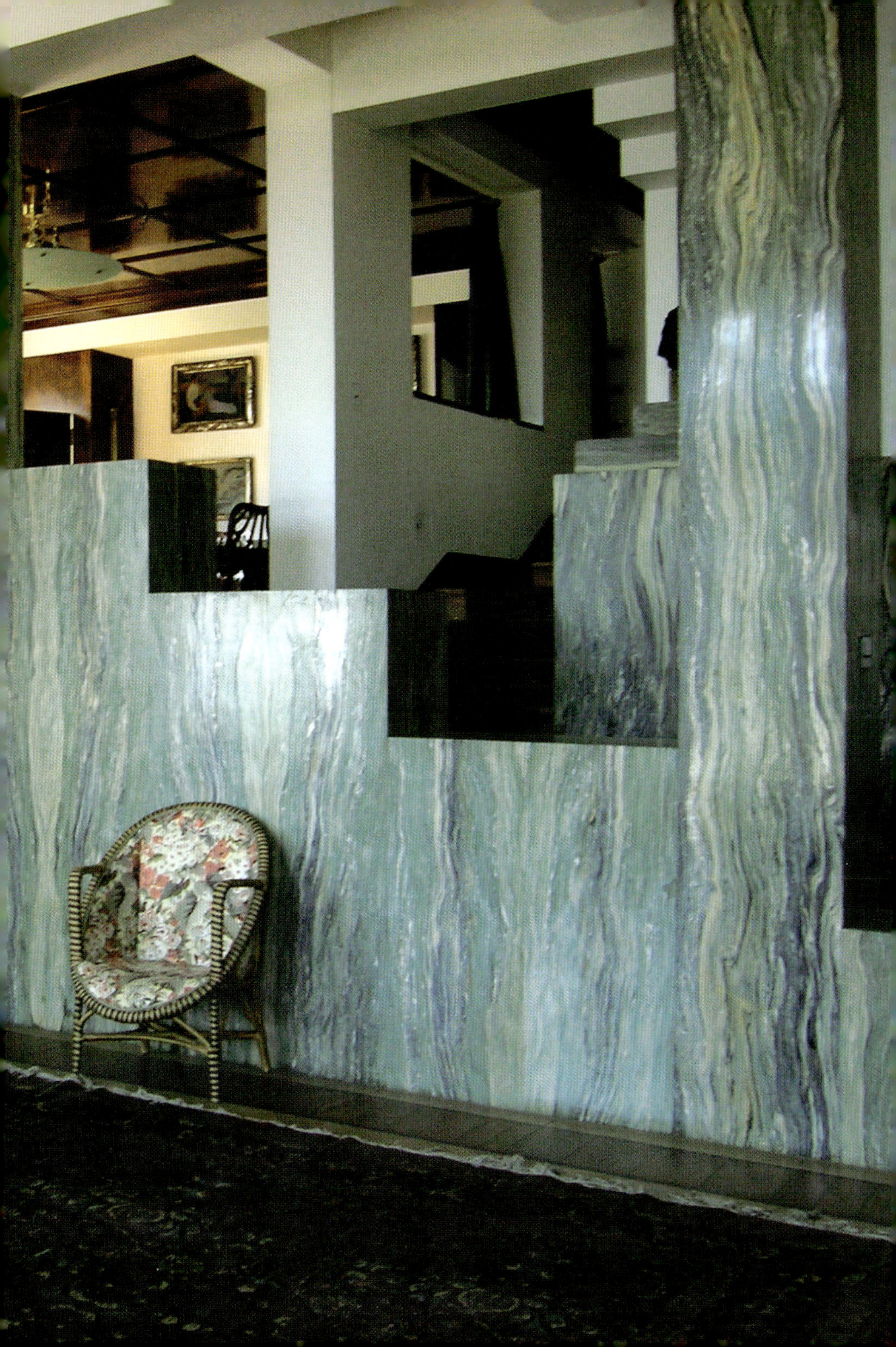

メイン・ホールのベンチ・ソファ。暖炉の対面にあって、これも左右対称の構成である。掛けられてある絵画も竣工当時のもの。この絵画の三幅対の位置も、設計時のロースによる指示と思われる。アドルフ・ロースは竣工した1930年にここで60歳の誕生日をあげ、このベンチで記念撮影した写真が残っている。

Bench sofa of the main hall. This faces the fireplace and is set symmetrically as well. The pictures are from the time of the original completion of the building. The placement of three pictures is thought to have been directed by Loos. There remains a birthday picture of Loos which was taken when he was 60 years old. He is sitting on a bench back in 1930, when this building was completed.

中央の凹みには、下階の前室からあがってくる階段が隠されている。天井高の低い凹みから突如二層分の大きなメイン・ホールへと出る。

There is a hidden stairway from the front chamber downstairs in the hollow in the center of the room. You come out of the hollow with a low ceiling into the main hall which has a height of two floors.

チポリーノの分厚い壁の隙間からメイン・ホールを左手に見ながら、ダイニング・ルームへとあがっていく。メインホールとダイニング・ルームを分ける壁は、その厚みをわざと強調するようにして段々状にセットバックしている。ダイニング・ルームは、マホガニーの深い木目の格天井が特徴的な部屋である。メイン・ホールと視覚的にはつながっていても、室ごとに仕上げの素材を変えている。

Going up to the dining room while looking at the main hall to the left through the thick cipollino wall. The thickness of the wall is intentionally emphasized and the wall gradually recedes to the top. The dining room is unique with the lacquer of dark mahogany wood-graining. The finishing materials used in these rooms (the main hall and the dining room) are different. Yet, the dining room is visually connected to the main hall.

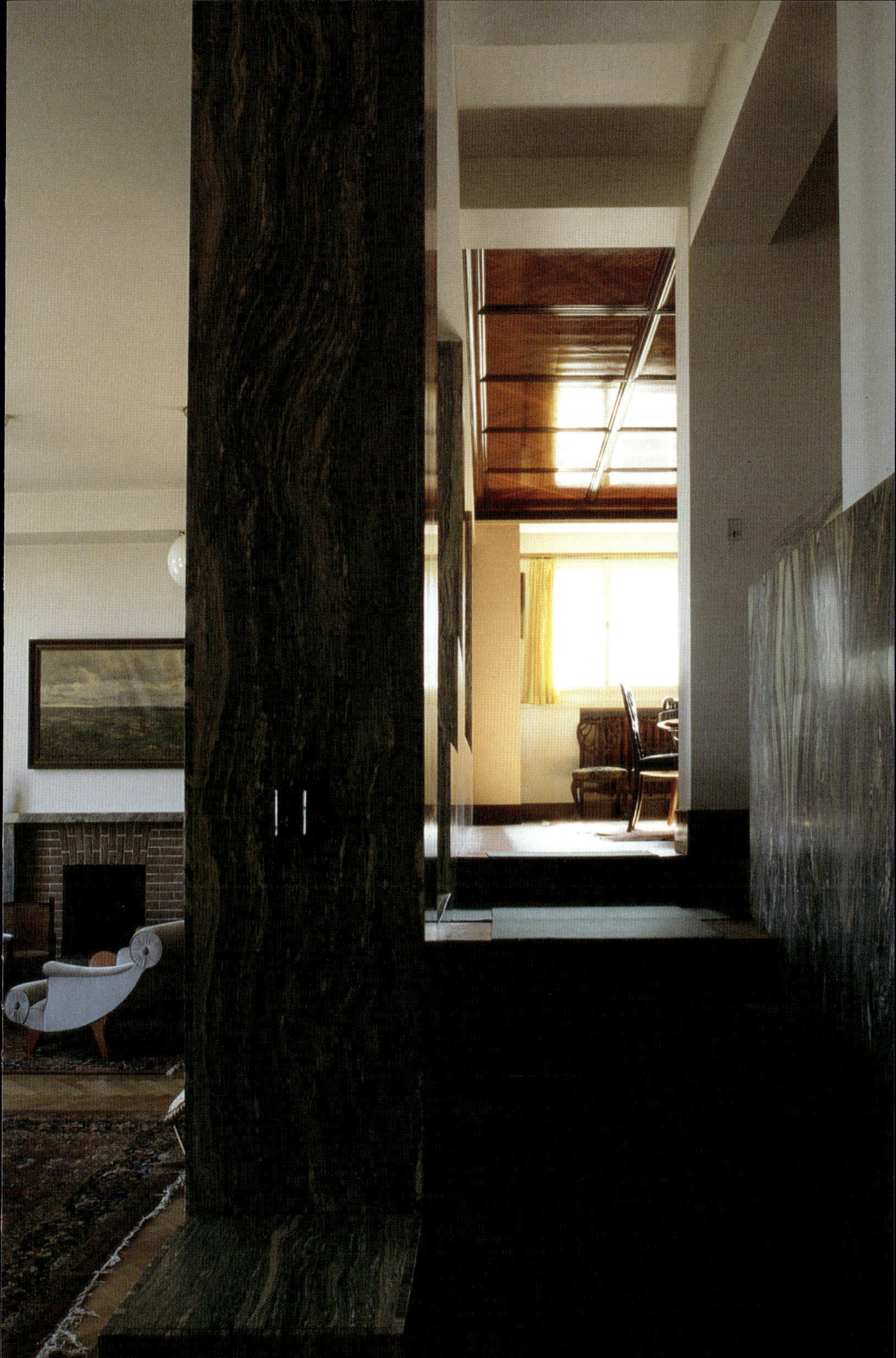

▲ ダイニング・ルームからメイン・ホールをのぞむ。チポリーノの壁が林立する垂直性の強い空間であることがよくわかる。
Looking at the main hall from the dining room. This space has a strong sense of verticality with standing cipollino walls.

▲ ダイニング・ルーム。巨大な円形テーブルを囲む。マホガニーの仕上げ材で全体的に落ち着いた雰囲気を醸し出している。メインホールとの境に腰壁が立ち上がっており、ダイニングテーブルに着席すると、メイン・ホールとの視線が切れるようになっている。

Dining room. With a large round table in the center, the whole atmosphere is solemn with mahogany finishing. When you sit at the dining table, the sight line to the main hall is cut off by the short walls that cross between the rooms.

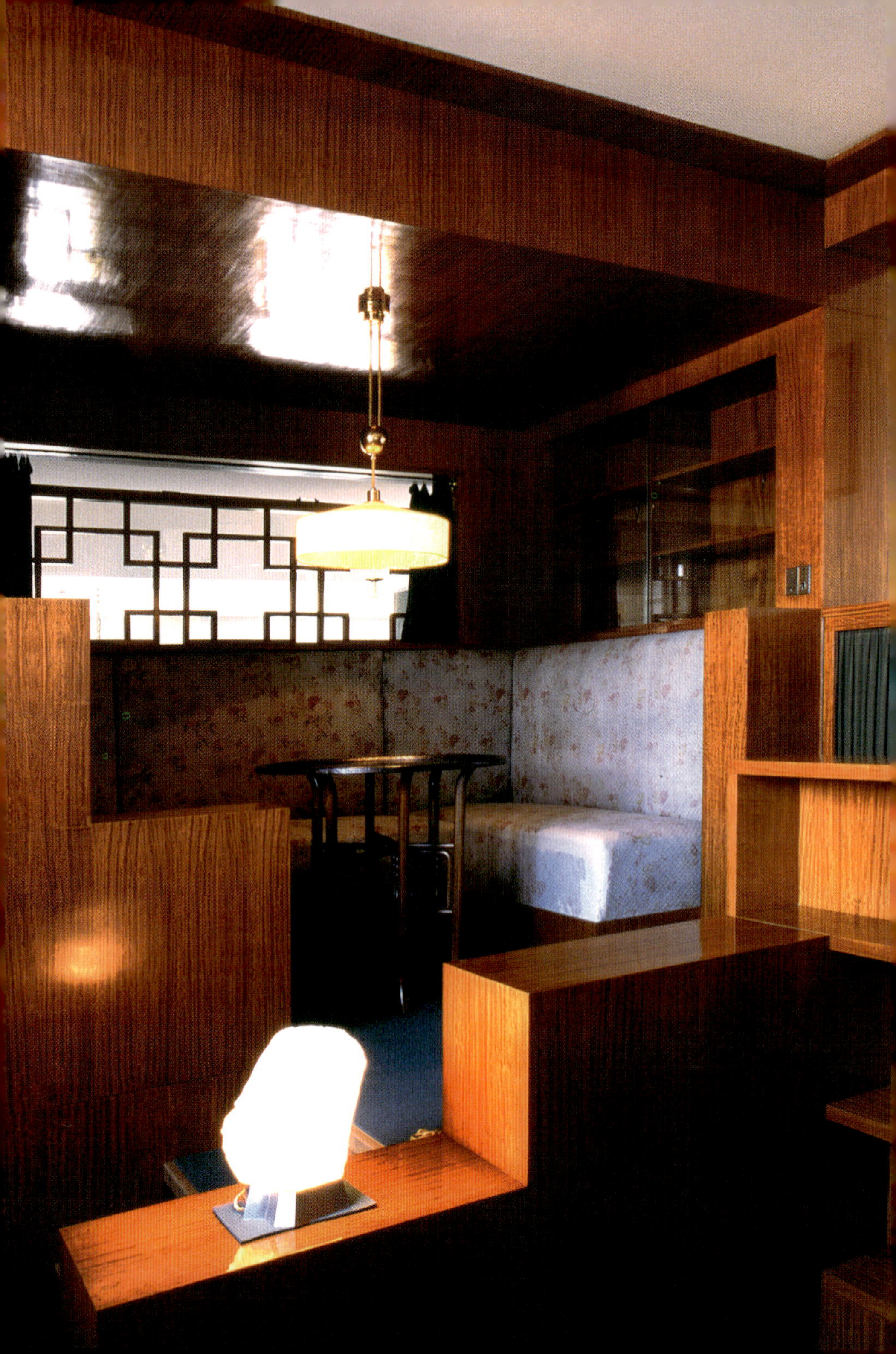

婦人室。メイン・ホールからダイニング・ルームと反対の方向の階段をあがっていくと、この婦人室にたどりつく。ここは面積はとても小さいのだが、レベル差と収納壁、壁の凹みなどを巧みに利用して、婦人がプライヴェートにくつろげるさまざまなシチュエーションを提供している。ミュラー婦人の身体寸法にぴったりと合ったオーダーメイドの空間。家具の組み合わせでできあがったような空間である。

Boudoir. Walk up the stairway from the main hall in the opposite direction of the dining room, and you will reach this boudoir. This room offers many opportunities for ladies' private relaxation because of different levels, storage walls, and alcoves in the wall. Furniture is custom-made per the measure of Mrs. Muller. This boudoir is like a combination of furniture forming a room.

書斎。ダイニング・ルームと同じくマホガニーで仕上げられ、深く落ち着いた空間である。狭さを補うように暖炉の上部に鏡が貼られていて、奥へと続いている錯覚をひきおこす。アメリカン・バーの内装など他の作品でも、鏡を使って視覚的に空間を拡張していく方法はしばしば試みられている。

Library. The library is a peaceful space finished with mahogany, the same as the dining room. Mirrors are set above the fireplace to alleviate the modest size of the room; hence, you may experience the sensory illusion that the room appears larger than it really is. Loos often attempted these visual enlargements of spaces with mirrors; such as his work in the American bar.

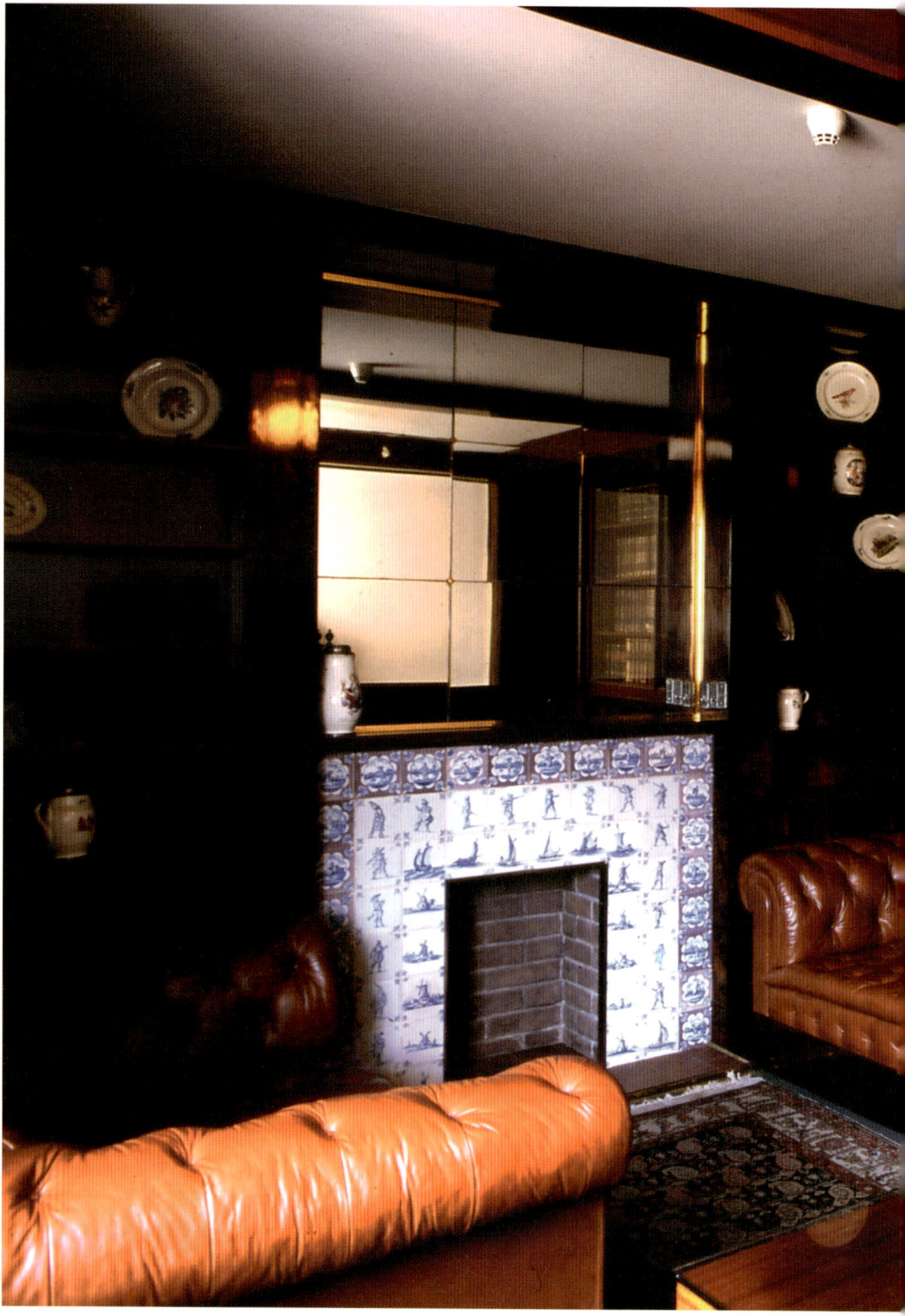

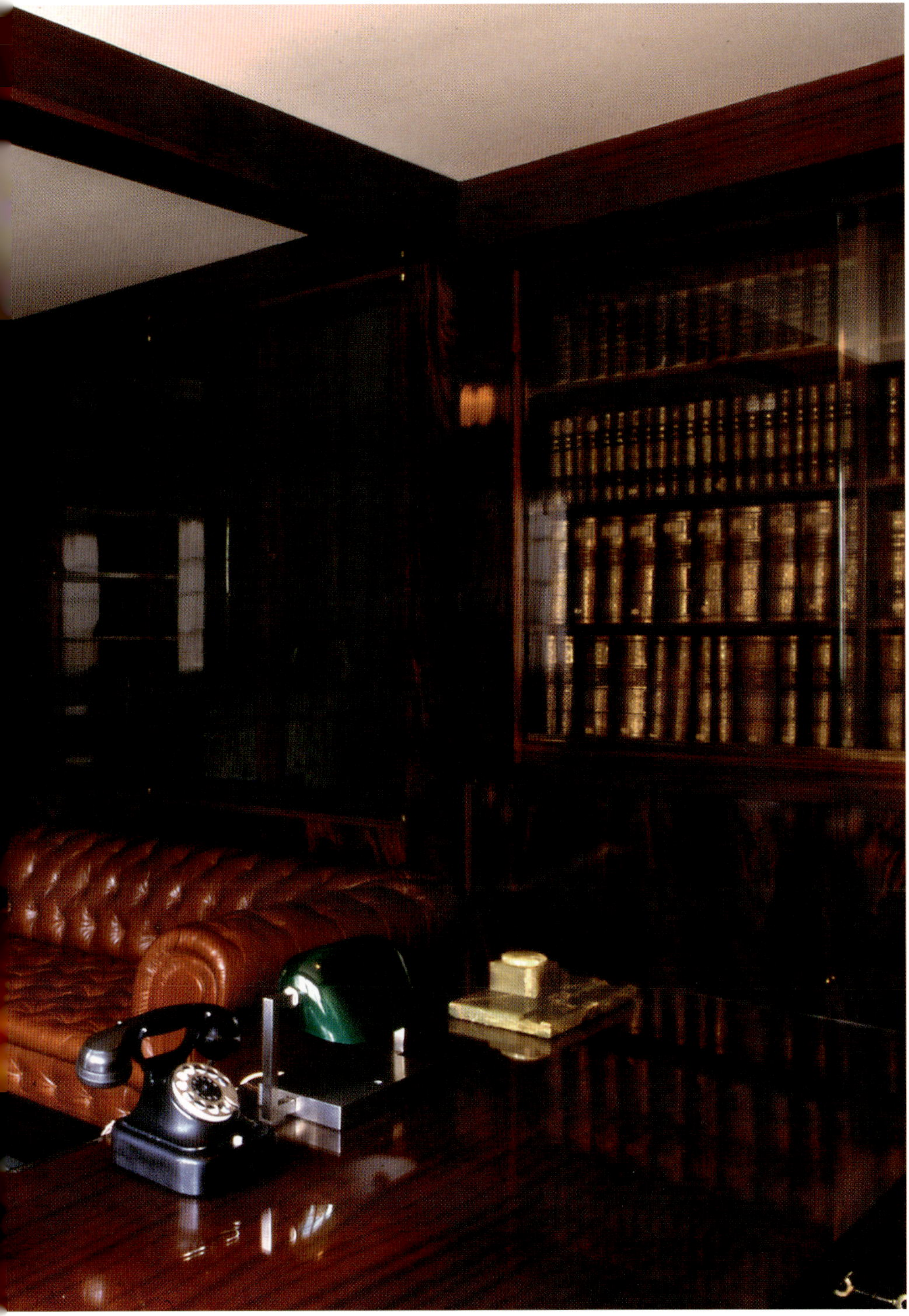

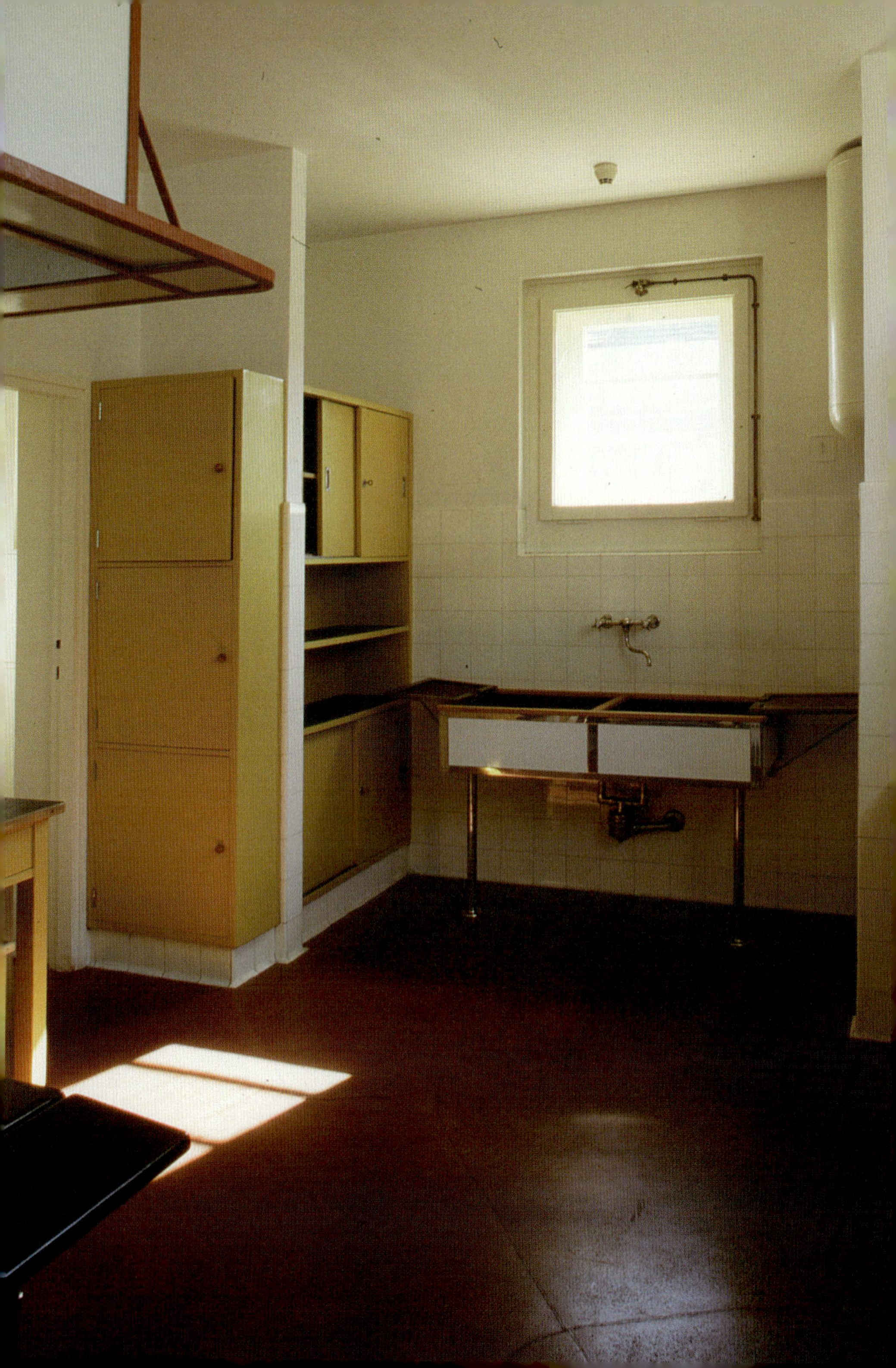

▲ バス・ルーム。イギリス製の衛生器具が採用されている。洗面器なども二つ対になって設置されている。

Bathroom. The sanitary appliances are made in England. The basins are set as a pair.

◀ キッチン。キッチンはダイニング・ルームとはうって変わって、白と黄色で塗装された明るく機能的な場所である。

Kitchen. Totally different from the dining room, the kitchen is a light and functional space painted white and yellow.

▲ 子供用寝室。子供には寝室とプレイ・ルームが続き部屋で用意されている。子供のための空間は青と黄色の塗装が大胆に用いられてとても明るい。寝室とプレイ・ルームとでは青と黄色の色使いを反転させて変化をつけている。

Children's room. The bedroom and the children's playroom are connected. The spaces for children are audaciously painted light blue and yellow. The use of blue and yellow is different in comparison to the bedroom.

女性用ワードローブ・ルーム。主寝室の両側には、男性用と女性用のワードローブ・ルームがそれぞれ設けられている。女性用には、窓辺に化粧台がある。

Lady's dressing room. On both sides of the main bedroom, there are dressing rooms for gentlemen and ladies respectively. The lady's dressing room has a dresser by the window.

▲ 主寝室。主寝室は北東に小さなテラスがついており、プラハ市街を見下ろす眺めのよい部屋である。壁には具象的な模様の壁紙が採用されている。

Main bedroom. This is a room with a view of Prague city and a small terrace to the northeast. The wallpaper has an objective pattern.

サマー・ブレックファスト・ルーム。六階の屋上テラスに隣接した外部性の強い部屋で、日本風の意匠が施されている。壁面の浮世絵は、竣工当時からのもの。

Summer breakfast room. This room is next to the outdoor rooftop terrace on the 6th floor and has a strong connection to the outside. The room has a Japanese style of decoration, and the Ukiyoe on the wall from the original completion of the building.

屋上テラス。奥にサマー・ブレックファスト・ルームがあり、地続きでテラスにでることができる。下の階段室に光をおとすトップライトが中央に見える。

Rooftop terrace. To the rear is the summer breakfast room which is connected to the terrace. In the center are top lights for the downstairs staircase.

北西ファサード
六階の屋上には自立壁が立ち上がって、屋上のプライヴァシーを保っているが、北東側に向けて壁が欠き取られて、眺望に開かれている。

Northwest façade. There is a standing wall on the rooftop of the 6th floor which allows for privacy. The wall of the northeast corner has been opened to allow for a view.

▲ 西側から見る夜景。外に対して寡黙で、中の様子をうかがい知ることは難しい。内部空間の複雑なレベル操作も、外からはよくわからないようになっている。仮面としての外被。装飾のないのっぺらぼうの表情が印象的である。

Night view from the west. The villa is not open to the outside and it is difficult to know what is inside. It is impossible to tell that there are complex level differences within the interior spaces. The outer walls act as a mask. It impressively hides the complex interior with an expressionless face, sans fancy decorations.

Section

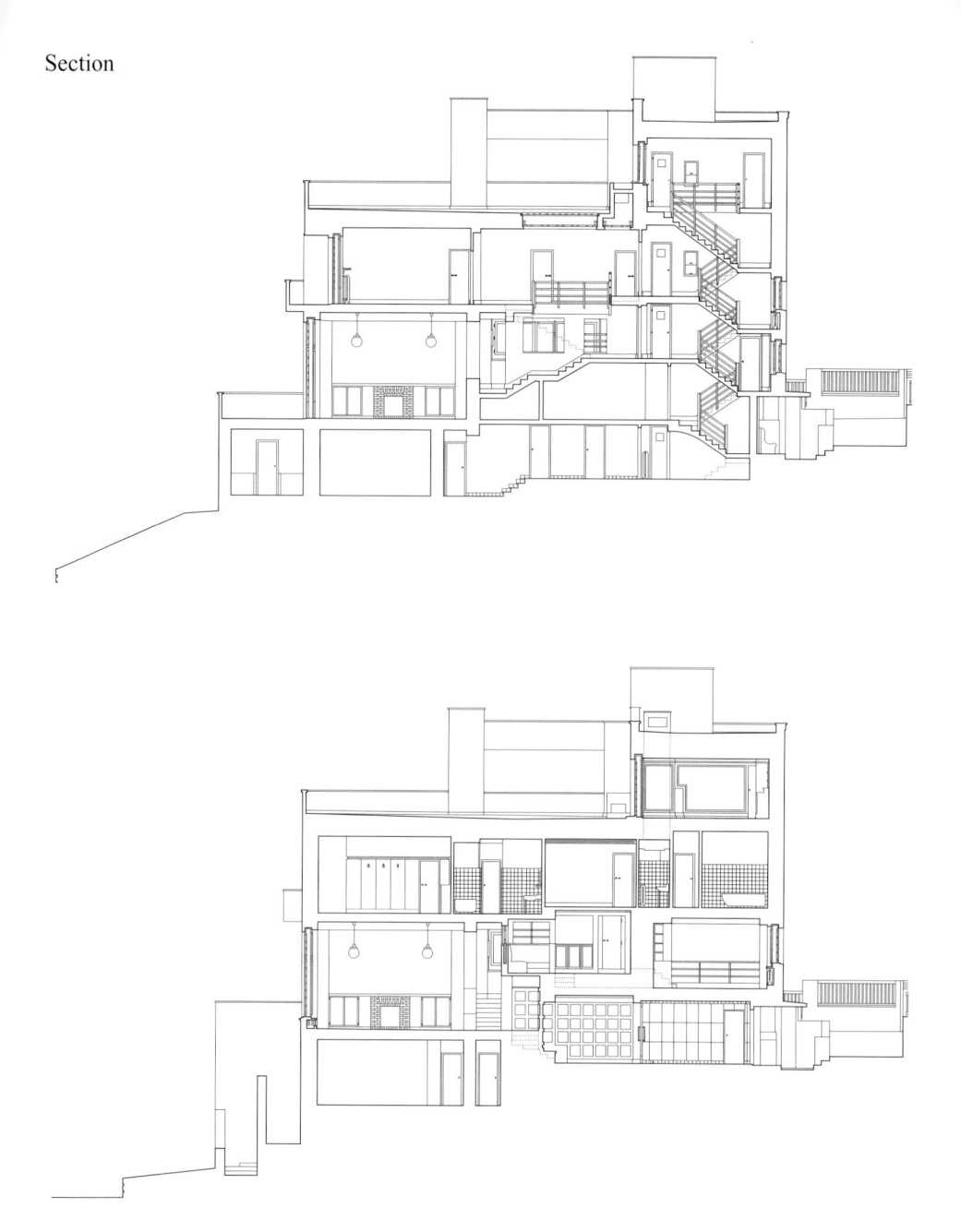

建物の中心部分に縦動線の階段を集約させることで、複雑なレベル差があるにもかかわらず、無駄な動線を省くことができている。階段を中心にらせん状のうごきが生まれて、らせんからはじき出されるようにして、個々の部屋に入っていく。また複数ある階段をたくみに配置して、主動線とサービス動線をきれいに分けている。
撮影：畑 拓（彰国社）

Needless circulations are avoided by concentrating stairways in the center of the house, although there are complex level differences. There is a spiral flow within the building and you will enter into each room as if you have fallen out of the spiral. Main and service circulations are clearly divided by the careful allocation of several stairways. Photo by Taku Hata(Shokokusha)

ミュラー邸
建築家：アドルフ・ロース
竣工：1930年
主体構造：RC造
延床面積：906m^2
各階面積：1F/264m^2 2F/216m^2
　　　　　3F/144m^2 4F/216m^2
　　　　　5F/66m^2
住所：Stresovice820, Prague

Villa Muller
Architect: Adolf Loos
Completed in 1930
Main Structure: RC structure
Total Floor Area:906m^2
Each Floor Area: 1F/264m^2 2F/216m^2
*　　　　　　　 3F/144m^2 4F/216m^2*
*　　　　　　　 5F/66m^2*
Address:Stresovice820, Prague

Elevation

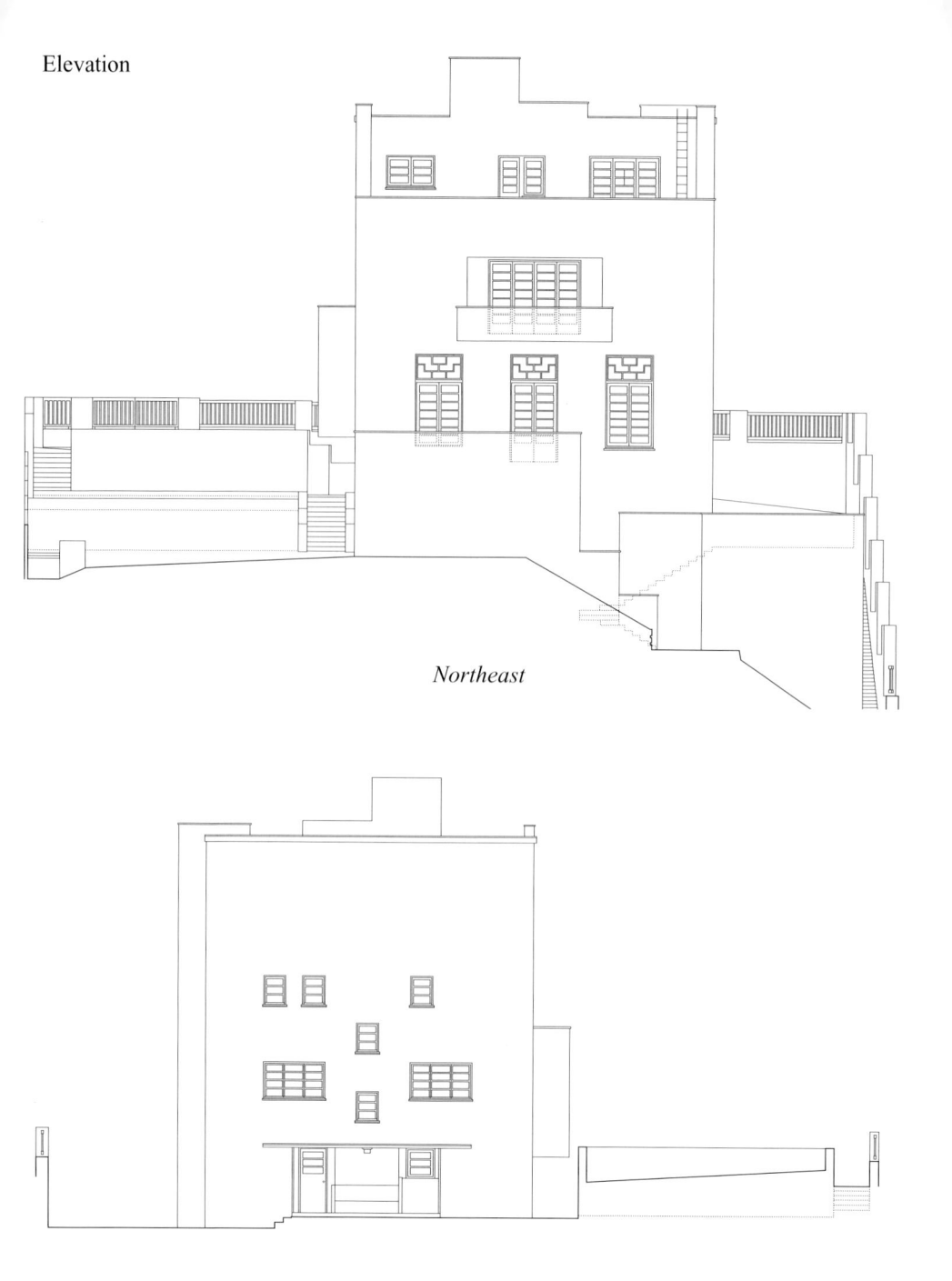

Northeast

Southwest

Northwest

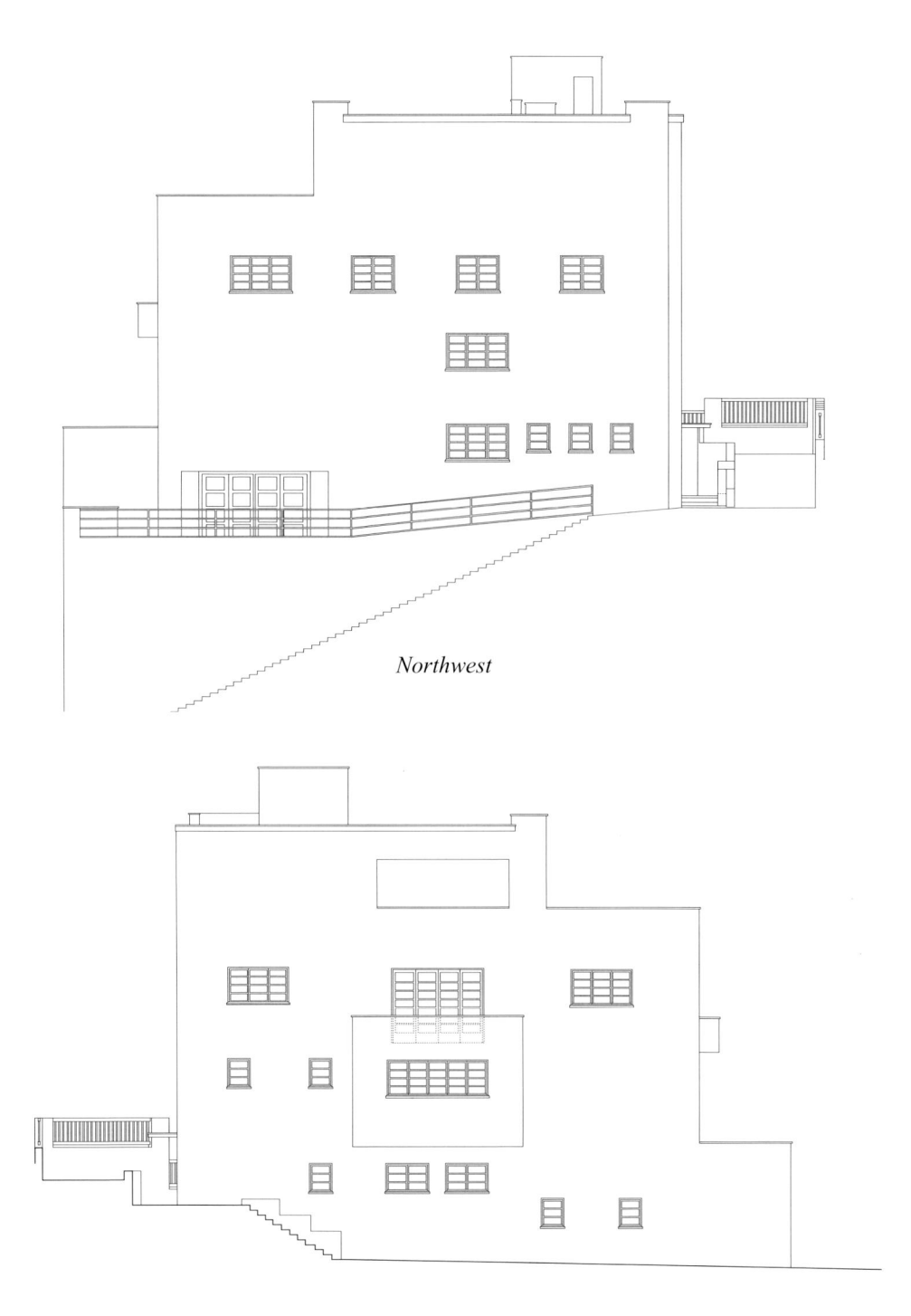

Southeast

アドルフ・ロースの現代性

装飾はいらない：生活の多様性へ

　装飾は犯罪である。自分のからだに刺青をするのは変質者か犯罪者であって、それと同じように建物に装飾をほどこすのは、犯罪である。建築家アドルフ・ロースは、こんなセンセーショナルなことばを残している。このことばの強く扇動的なニュアンスが広く知られることによって彼は、装飾を否定して無機的な近代建築をはじめたといわれている。たしかにアドルフ・ロースが設計した建物は、外側から見るかぎりではのっぺらぼうで素っ気なく、19世紀までの西欧の様式的な建物に比べると無表情である。しかし、建物を無機的に味気なくデザインすることがアドルフ・ロースの意図だったわけではない。彼の装飾批判の向かうところは別のところにあった。

　アドルフ・ロースが生きた19世紀末のウィーンでは、室内空間に装飾をあふれさせてあらゆるものの表面を装飾で埋めつくそうとするデザインが流行していた。アドルフ・ロースにとって装飾とは、一つの様式できれいに統一された飾りで室内を満たすことである。こうした装飾の何が、ロースにとっては問題だったのだろうか。

　統一された様式は、それ自体で完結している。照明器具からベッドの脚、壁紙から手摺にいたるまで、同じ様式で統一しなければ気がすまない。どんどん装飾が繁殖していく。そしてそんな装飾の統一性のなかに自分も同一化して満足感を覚える。こんな偏執的な装飾は、ちょうど刺青で皮膚の表面を覆いつくそうとする欲望にも似て、病的である。19世紀末の装飾は文化的な装いをしているけれども、その根底にあるのは原始的な欲望なのだとロースは暴き立てた。

　自分の顔を飾りたてたり身の回りのものすべてに装飾をほどこしたいという衝動が、造形芸術の起源だった。エロティックともいえるこのような衝動から芸術ははじまっている。だからロースは装飾が人間にとっての基本的な欲望であることを認めている。しかし、そのような偏執的で原始的な欲望のままに近代を生き抜くことは許されない。装飾に頼らず、装飾にかたむけた欲望や労力を他のことに向けたほうが生産的であろう。無装飾であることの潔さ。ロースにとって、無装飾は精神的な強さのしるしなのである。装飾は犯罪であるというロースの扇動的なことばは、こんな背景のなかから出てきたものである。

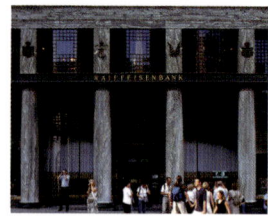

●ロース・ハウス
1911年竣工。ウィーンのミヒャエル広場に建つこのロース・ハウスは、外観の装飾を排したため建設当時、批判の対象となった。現在では、初期の現代建築の道標的役割を果たしたとして評価されている。

Looshaus
Completed in 1911, the Looshaus, located at the Michaelerplatz, Vienna, was criticized at the time of its completion because of its lack of outside decorations. This building is now esteemed as a signpost for early modern architecture.

Modernity of Adolf Loos

Ornament is Unnecessary: toward a Variety of Life

Ornament is a crime. Somebody with a tattoo might be a psychopath or a criminal and it would, thus, be a crime to decorate buildings. Thus, the architect, Adolf Loos, left those sensational phrases. Since these strong and agitating nuanced phrases were widely known, he established his reputation as a pioneer of inorganic modern architecture denying ornament. The buildings he designed, for sure, are free of decoration and brusque compared to the other Western styled buildings up until the 19th century. His intention was, however, not to merely design buildings which were inorganic and brusque. He was criticizing decorations for another purpose.

In Adolf LoosÁe time, the 19th century, interior designs full of decorations were quite popular. Ornament was, for Loos, filling the indoor spaces with decorations of one unified style. Why did such decorations seem so wrong to him?

A unified style is self-contained. Everything should be covered with the same style; the lighting equipment, bed legs, wallpapers and handrails. Decorations became more and more rampant. One might, thereby, devote oneself into such a uniformity of decorations and be satisfied. Paranoiac ornament of this kind would be pathetic, just like a desire to cover ones skin with tattoos. Loos demonstrated that primitive desires were actually the driving force of ornament in the 19th century, which appeared to have culture on the surface.

The origin of figurative arts came from desires to decorate our faces and all the things around us. Art was possibly originated from these erotic passions. Hence, Loos admits that ornaments are merely a basic lust of human beings. It is, yet, not forgivable to live with such paranoiac and primitive wants in this modern age. It would be more productive to put such efforts towards other things, not just towards decorations. Grace is to be found in being non-decorative. For Loos, bareness is a token of mental strength. His agitating phrases emerged from the background of ornament as a crime.

Miscellaneous objects encroach into modern life. It is, in particular, the age when various consumer goods are eating daily life in accordance with the rise of capitalism. The stylistic life can be attained if we can have all the daily commodities within one style. Such a way is, however, not allowed anymore in modern life. Interior spaces are full of heterogeneous things. Decorations should have been wiped out once and for all so that we can face inevitable modern situations.

A house organized under one unified style ties up its residents. The style becomes more important than the residents in such a

アメリカン・バー
1908年竣工のアドルフ・ロース設計によるバー。平面は、4.45メートル x 6.15メートル足らずのとても小さなバーで、ベンチシートを使って人の身体を包み込むようなつくりになっているが、壁面上部は鏡貼りで格天井を映し出し、どこまでも空間が広がっていくような錯覚を引き起こしている。

American Bar
Designed by Adolf Loos and completed in 1908. It is a very small bar of about 4.45m x 6.15m with bench seats that envelop the human body. Since the mirrors at the upper side of the walls reflect the lacquer, you experience a sensory illusion that this space continues without limit.

近代の生活にはさまざまな雑多なものが侵入してくる。まして資本主義の発達にともなって、多種多様な消費物資が日常生活を侵食しはじめた時代である。すべての身の回りのものをその様式で揃えていくことができるのならば、様式的な生活にもリアリティはあるだろう。しかしもう近代の生活ではそういうわけにはいかなくなってきていた。さまざまな異質なものたちであふれかえる室内。避けがたいこの近代的な状況に正面から向き合うためには、装飾をいったんきれいにクリアランスする必要があった。

　一つの様式で統一された部屋は、住み手をしばりつける。そこでは主役は様式であって住み手ではない。住み手は様式に合うかどうかで新たに買う物を決める必要があって、その様式にふさわしい暮らしをすることが求められる。住宅は誰のものだろうか。アドルフ・ロースは問いかける。住み手のものである。この当たり前の答えは、後の近代建築家であるル・コルビュジエやミース・ファン・デル・ローエならば絶対に口にしなかったであろうことばである。住宅は住み手が自分でつくりあげるものである。住み手が自分の痕跡を刻みつけて、他でもない自分の部屋を作りだしていく。こうした住み手の行為を可能にするフォーマットを、建築家は設計することになるのである。生活の多様性を受け入れる器を模索すること。これは、とても現代的な問いでもある。ロースの装飾批判の向かう先は、実はここにあった。

平面図はいらない：ラウムプランへ

　生活の多様性を受け入れるための場をつくりだすために、ロースは独特の設計手法を生み出していく。「ラウムプラン」と呼ばれることになるロースの考え方は、決定的に新しい一歩を建築の歴史に刻み込んでいくことになった。では、「ラウムプラン」とはどのようなものだろうか。それは、住宅の部屋割りを従来のように各階ごとに平面で考えるのではなく、三次元の空間、立体において考えることである。将来はチェスを三次元の立体格子において遊び興ずることが可能になるのと同じようにして、三次元の空間を直接操作して住宅を計画することになるだろう、とロースは言う。

　三次元のチェス。想像しただけで気が遠くなりそうだ。二次元のチェスでも、そのオペレーションは複雑なのに、それが三

situation. The residents should determine whether or not they can adjust themselves to that style before they buy the house and are forced to live in within the style. Adolf Loos asks, "To whom does a house belong?". It belongs to its residents. Although this is a natural answer, later modern architects, like Le Corbusier or Mies van der Rohe, would never answer that way. The residents create their own house. They leave their traces in customizing their own rooms. Architects are to design with a format that enables the residents' such activities. To pursue for a container to accommodate a variety of life. This is also a very contemporary issue. What Loos criticized was actually directed to handle such kind of matters.

Plans are Unnecessary: toward Raumplan

Loos invented his original ways of designing spaces to accept a variety of life. His ideas, called "raumplan," made a benchmark in the history of architecture. What was, then, "raumplan"? It is to think of the room layout of houses as a three-dimensional figure, instead of individual floor plans in a conventional way. Loos says, in the future, we should design a house through direct control of three dimensional spaces; just like playing chess in a three-dimensional grid.

Chess of three-dimension. How complex would chess be in three-dimension since it is already complicated in the two-dimensional grid? Architecture is based upon two dimensional planar concepts. In most cases, one thinks of layouts through drawing plans and then determines elevations and sections by first providing information on height. Loos says, however, such a way is only a combination of two dimensional concepts. For example, Michelangelo of the Renaissance

次元に展開したら一体どうなるのだろう。建築は平面的な二次元の思考に基づいている。設計をするときも人は、だいたい平面図を描きながら間取りを決めて、そこに高さ情報を与えて立面や断面を決めていくことが多い。しかしそれでは、二次元をただ組み合わせたことにしかならないとロースは言う。たとえば、ルネサンス時代の彫刻家ミケランジェロは、平面的に彫刻や建築を構想していなかった。彼は対象をあらゆる角度から同時に見据えて直接空間そのものを操作していた。同じように近代の建築家は、空間を直接三次元的につくりだすことが必要なのだ。ちょうど同じ頃、ロースの友人であったアーノルト・シェーンベルク※1という音楽家がいた。彼は伝統的な調性をこわして十二音技法を開発したことで知られるが、それはロースが空間に関しておこなったこととてもよく似ている。

長年にわたってロースの協力者であったハインリッヒ・クルカ※2が編集した作品集のなかで、クルカはラウムプランの概念を解説している。その最初の適用例として、1919年のシュトラッサー邸※3と1922年のルーファー邸※4が取り上げられている。ルーファー邸の設計で描かれた立面図はかなり特殊なものである。開口部は窓枠とガラスの表現がされるかわりに黒く塗りつぶされている。ファサードの輪郭線に加えて、破線によって内部のスラブや壁体の位置が描き込まれている。つまりここでは透明なものが物質感をともなって描かれていて、逆にマッシブ

※1 **アーノルト・シェーンベルク**
音楽家。オーストリア生まれ。1874-1951。調性を脱し、無調音楽に入る12音技法を創始したことで知られる。アドルフ・ロースと親交が深かったことでも知られる。

※1 **Arnold Schönberg**
Composer. Born in Austria. 1874-1951. Arnold Schönberg, known as the creator of twelve-tone music was also known as a close acquaintance of Adolf Loos.

※3 **シュトラッサー邸**
1919年にウィーンに竣工した住宅で、既存の建物改築である。二層分の天井高の音楽室の一角に床を設けて演奏スペースと書斎を設けた。

※3 **Villa Strasser**
Residence completed in 1919 in Vienna, it was renovated from an existing building. A floor was installed into a part of the music room with a height of two floors and created both a playing and a reading space.

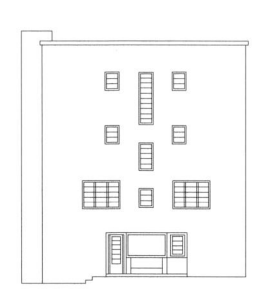

1. 当初の案では、階段室の場所を暗示させ、内部空間のプライヴァシーの度合いを反映させた窓のデザインになっている。

1. The original design of the windows implies the staircase and reflects the degree of privacy in the inner spaces.

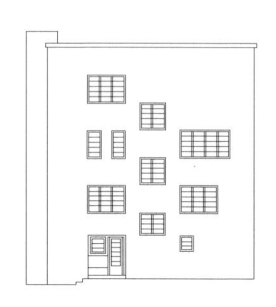

2. 階段室と居室の窓を同じにして、違いが分からないようになってきている。正面にあったエントランスを窓のスケールに合わせている。

2. There is no clear borderline between the windows of the staircase and the other rooms. The entrance, which previously was in the center, is now adjusted to the scale of the windows.

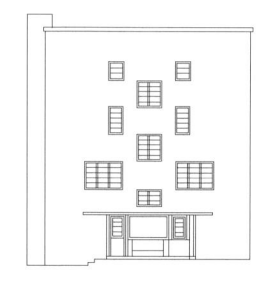

3. 左右対称の均整のとれたプロポーションへと修正しようとしている。エントランスが元に戻っている。

3. Attempting to create symmetrical and balanced proportions, the entrance has been reverted back to its original location.

*²ハインリッヒ・クルカ
チェコスロヴァキア生まれの建築家。1900年－1971年。ウィーンで建築を学んだ後、アドルフ・ロースの下で働き、後に協働者となる。ロースの最初の作品集を出版している。

*² **Heinrich Kulka**
Heinrich Kulka was an architect born in Czechoslovakia. 1900-1971. After studying architecture in Vienna, he worked under Adolf Loos and later became his co-worker. He published the first works of Loos.

*⁴ ルーファー邸
1922年にウィーンに竣工した住宅。10メートルキューブの外殻を耐力壁として中央に一本煙突を内蔵した柱をつくり、それ以外を木造の非耐力壁にすることで、自由な立体的空間を作り出すことに成功している。

*⁴ **Rufer House**
House completed in Vienna in 1922. This building successfully has free stereoscopic spaces with the outer bearing walls of 10m cubed and the central column with a chimney in it. Other walls are wooden and non-bearing.

age did not conceptualize sculptures or architecture planarly. He directly constructed spaces by watching the object from every angle at the same time. As such, modern architects should create spaces directly and three-dimensionally. Arnold Schönberg*¹, a composer and friend of Loos, is famous in that he invented twelve-tone music by overcoming traditional tonality. This is similar to what Loos did to spaces.

Heinrich Kulka*², a co-worker of Loos for a long time, illustrates the concepts of raumplan in the publication he edited. He picks up the Villa Strasser*³ in 1919 and the Rufer House*⁴ in 1922 as the first applications of raumplan. The elevations of the Rufer House are particularly unique. The door openings are painted black instead of being expressed like the window frames and glass. Inner slabs and walls are drawn with broken lines as well as the façade line. That is, transparent materials are expressed with materiality and, in reverse; massive walls are transparent to some extent and show what are inside. The elevation shows what you can see from the outside. The inside and outside, and the elevation and the sections are, however, expressed at the same time here. The same kind of study was attempted in the drawings of the Villa Muller. The dense and compressed feelings of the inner spaces of Loos' buildings are attributed to such processes of design.

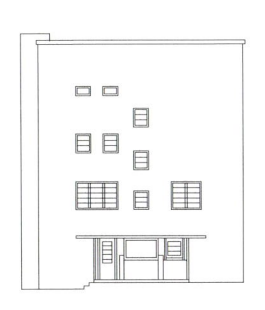

4. 上層階の窓を減らしている。エントランスに庇をつけて水平線を強調し、全体的に重心を低くしようとしている。

4. Decreasing the windows of the upper side. The total barycenter is lower with a horizontal emphasis of the entrance eaves.

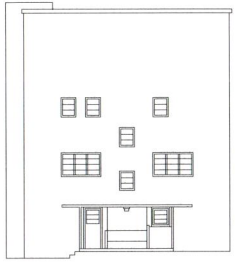

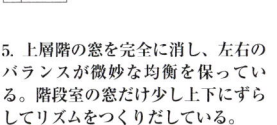

5. 上層階の窓を完全に消し、左右のバランスが微妙な均衡を保っている。階段室の窓だけ少し上下にずらしてリズムをつくりだしている。

5. The windows of the upper side have been completely erased. This maintains a balance on the edge between the right and the left. Vertical displacements of the staircase windows have a rhythm.

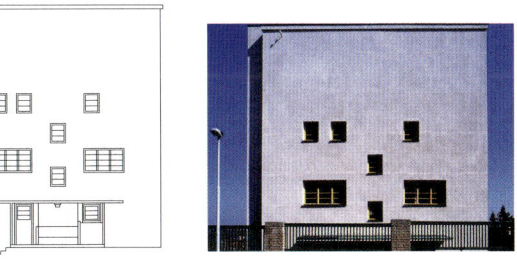

な壁体がなかば透明で、内側のものをすかし見せるように描かれている。立面図は外部から見た視点に映るものを描くものだが、ここでは外部と内部、立面と断面とが同時に露呈している。同じようなスタディは、のちのミュラー邸においても試みられている。ロースの内部空間に密度感があって圧縮された感覚を抱かせるのは、こうした設計プロセスのおかげであろう。

　シュトラッサー邸は既存の建物の改築である。最初にラウムプランが適用されたのが改築だというのは興味深い。ロースは天井高の高いこの住宅の玄関ホールに中二階のレヴェルを挿入することを思いつく。シュトラッサー邸ではロースは、書斎と音楽室のアルコーブを設けることになったが、天井高を低くできるアルコーブの存在がロースのラウムプランにおいて鍵になる役割を担わされたようだ。アルコーブとホールの関係について、ロースは演劇ホールと桟敷席との関係を引いて説明している。桟敷席は親密な空間だが、舞台を見ると同時に客席からも見られる関係にある。ロースは、このような劇場的な関係性を住宅のなかに取り入れようとした。こうしたロースのラウムプランが、最も成熟したかたちで実現したのが、ミュラー邸である。

統一性はいらない：ミュラー邸へ

　アドルフ・ロースは、1870年に現在のチェコスロヴァキア、ブルノで生まれた。ドレスデンで建築学校をでたあとアメリカで放浪生活を送り、その後26歳のときにヨーロッパに戻り、ウィーンに定住する。1923年にはウィーンからパリに移り、1928年に再度ウィーンに戻っている。

　一方、施主となるフランティシェク・ミュラーはピルセンを拠点にした大きな土木建設会社の跡取りとして生まれた。1920年代のなかばには、ミュラー氏はピルセンからチェコスロヴァキアの首都プラハに拠点をうつす。1928年の秋、ミュラー氏は、アドルフ・ロースとその共働者であったカレル・ロータに、プラハに住宅を設計するように依頼する。アドルフ・ロースはウィーンに事務所を構えていたが、当時ロースの事務所にスタッフはいなかった。そこでチェコの建築学校で教えていたカレル・ロータは、チェコでのロースの仕事を手伝うことになったのである。

　ミュラー邸は、1929年12月31日に竣工し、翌年の夏からミュ

The Villa Strasser is a renovation of an existing building. It is interesting that the first adaptation of raumplan was a renovation. Loos came up with an idea that a mezzanine floor should be inserted into the entrance hall of the house to create a middle level since the ceiling had such a considerable height. Regarding the Villa Strasser, Loos added library and music room alcoves. The existence of alcoves, which can have a lower height, would have played an important role in raumplan. Loos explains the relationships between the alcoves and the hall with reference to box-seats in a theater hall. The purpose of a box-seat, a very intimate space, is to watch the stage and at the same time, be watched by the audience seats. Loos attempted to restage such dramatic relationships in the house. Raumplan of this kind was realized in a most blossoming way at the Villa Muller.

Uniformity is Unnecessary: toward the Villa Muller

Adolf Loos was born in Brno, Czechoslovakia in 1870. He graduated from the school of architecture and then traveled around the USA. Then he came back to Europe at the age of 26 and settled down in Vienna. Loos moved to Paris in 1923 and came back to Vienna again in 1928.

Frantisek Muller, the future client, was born as an heir of a large construction company based in Pilsen. Mr. Muller moved his base from Pilsen to Prague, the capital of Czechoslovakia, in the middle of the 1920s. In fall, 1928, he asked Adolf Loos and his co-worker Karel Lhota to design a house for him in Prague. Adolf Loos did have an office in Vienna but there was no staff in the office at that time. That is why Karel Lhota, teaching at the architecture school in Czechoslovakia, was to help Loos' job in the country.

The Villa Muller was completed on the 31st December in 1929 and the Mullers started living in the villa the next summer. Adolf Loos, who turned 60 that year, had a birthday party in the main hall of the villa. Later, the Mullers stayed at the villa even when the Nazis invaded Bohemia. The villa came under surveillance by the government with the rise of communism. The villa was used as the

ラー一家はこの住宅に住みはじめる。ちょうどその年に還暦をむかえたアドルフ・ロースは、この住宅のメイン・ホールで誕生パーティを開いている。その後、ナチスドイツがボヘミアに侵攻した際にもミュラー一家はこの住宅に留まっていた。第二次世界大戦後の共産主義の台頭とともに、ミュラー邸は政府の管轄のもとにおかれ、応用美術博物館になったり、政府の出版局として使われた時期もあった。そのあいだミュラー家はこの家での居住を認められていたが、彼らの生活領域は書斎と婦人室に限られるなど、きわめて抑圧された環境にあったようである。フランティシェク・ミュラー氏はほどなく亡くなってしまうが、婦人は1968年に亡くなるまでこの住宅に住み続けることになったのである。そして現在は整備されて見学ができるようになっている。

　ミュラー邸を訪れてみよう。プラハ市街を見下ろす丘の斜面に立つミュラー邸は、外側からみると閉ざされた箱型の建物である。平滑な壁面に窓がぽつりと開いたその外観は、ロースのほかの建物と同じようにのっぺらぼうで、ずいぶんと周囲の非難を浴びたようである。しかし今では周辺に同じような建物が立ち並んでいて、全く違和感がない。むしろ特性がない建物のように見えてしまうから皮肉なものである。

　平面図と断面図を見比べてよく読みこんでみるとわかるように、ミュラー邸はとても複雑な構成になっている。天井高の高いメイン・ホールから屈みこむアルコーブまで、さまざまな高さの部屋がぎっしりと詰め込まれて、スパイラル状の動線に巻きついている。

　メイン・ホールにでる直前の階段室は、天井高がぎりぎりまで抑えられていて、メイン・ホールの天井高とのコントラストを強くつけているため、余計にメインホールが大きく感じられる。階段室の上には、婦人室のアルコーブが入っていて、座った状態で寛げるスペースだ。そこはちょうど劇場の天井桟敷と同じように、窓を開けるとメイン・ホールが下に見渡せるようになっていて、守られた小さな空間と開放的な大きな空間の対比がつくりだされている。

　婦人室の内部がとても素晴らしい。とても狭い部屋なのだが、さまざまなくつろぎ方ができるようになっていて、なおかつレベル差をたくみに利用して同じ室内でもくつろぐ場所どうしが見えないようになっているのだ。この部屋はミュラー婦人の身体寸法からスケールが決定されていて、彼女のからだの延長のような小さな部屋である。ロースの意図がもっともはっきりと

カフェ・ムゼウム
1899年にアドルフ・ロースがデザインしたカフェで、クリムトやシーレをはじめとした芸術家や文化人が集まり、いわゆるウィーン世紀末芸術文化の中心的な場として栄えた。

Café Museum
Café designed by Adolf Loos in 1899. It flourished as the center of the Viennese Modern Age culture, where artists and intellectuals such as Klimt and Schiele would gather.

Museum of Applied Arts or the printing bureau by the government. The Mullers were allowed to live in the house, yet their life was very limited; their residential areas were limited to the library and the boudoir. Frantisek Muller passed away soon after, but Mrs. Muller continued living in the villa until she died in 1968. The villa was restored and is now open to visitors.

Let us visit the Villa Muller. The villa, looking down upon Prague city from a hill, appears shut out from the outside. The appearance of flat walls and small windows looks expressionless; just like other buildings by Loos. They say the villa was criticized severely. The villa is, however, now surrounded by similar buildings and looks comfortable among them. Ironically, the villa does not really appear unique.

The Villa Muller is complexly composed, which you will notice if you carefully examine the plans and the sections of the villa. The building is full of rooms with various heights; such as the main hall with a lofty height and the alcoves that require you to bend down. These rooms surround the spiral circulation.

The staircase just before the main hall has a minimal height. The contrast is, consequently, extreme to the height of the main hall, which makes you feel as if the main hall is even larger. Above the staircase, there is an alcove for ladies to sit and relax. From this alcove, you can look down upon the main hall by opening the window just like a box-seat in a theater. There is a contrast between a small sheltered space and a large open space.

Splendid is the interior of the boudoir. Although this is a very small room, there are various spaces to relax. You cannot, in addition, see each other between the relaxation spaces due to a careful use of level variances. The scales of this room are determined per measure of Mrs. Muller. This is a small room just like an extension of her body. The intentions of Loos are most clearly expressed in this room.

あらわれている部屋である。

　五層目の階段室は、なぜか山小屋風である。ロースは別荘建築も多く手がけているからそれとのつながりがあるのだろう。古代ローマを思わせるようなメイン・ホールの荘厳な雰囲気から一転して、くつろいだ明るくウッディな空気が漂う。一つの住宅のなかで、これほど多様な雰囲気が合体している建築がほかにあるだろうか。最上階にあるサマー・ブレックファスト・ルームは、日本風の意匠でつくりだされた部屋※5である。ロースの発言のなかには日本の建築の間取りについて言及するものも残っているから、日本建築にも興味があったのだろう。ここはミュラー邸のなかではめずらしく外に対して開かれた部屋で、テラスと連続的につくられている。ひとが集まる天井高の高い大きな部屋から、からだの延長のような一人でくつろぐ婦人室や書斎、外部と一体化した東洋的な部屋、明るく活動的な子供室。さまざまな部屋がそれぞれの使われ方にふさわしい規模とテクスチャー、色調でつくられ、集合している。これがミュラー邸の魅力である。

※5『今日私たちは日本の影響にあるから、平面プランは遠心的なのである。家具は部屋の四隅に置かれる。部屋の中心が自由になる（動線）。』
(Heinrich Kulka, Adolf Loos-Das Werk des Architekten8Wien: Anton Schroll Verlag,1931)

※5 *"We are under the influences of Japan and therefore plans are centrifugal. Furniture is set at the corners of the room, allowing for free circulation."* Heinrich Kulka, Adolf Loos-Das Werk des Architekten8Wien: Anton Schroll Verlag,1931)

高価な素材はいらない：着衣のような建築へ

　「被覆の原理」と題された論文の中で主張しているように、ロースにとって建築は、まず何より肌触りがよく暖かくて居心地がよい織物で身体の四周を覆うことからはじまる。あくまで心地よい場をつくりだすことが建築の目的である。構造的骨組みなどは、そのあとからそれを支えるために考え出されればよいのだ。ル・コルビュジエが提唱したドミノ・システムに代表されるように、近代の建築は鉄やコンクリートという新しい素材が可能にした構法を出発点として思い描かれている。だからロースが建築を着衣のように考えて内側から考えるのは、前近代的にも見える。

　しかし、考えてみよう。「ラウムプラン」の考え方にもとづいて固定した床を自由に動かし、無駄のない変化に富んだ内部空間をつくりだすロース。それぞれの部屋にふさわしい高さをあたえて部屋どうしの組み合わせを考え、流れるようなつながりをもつ垂直的な空間を、彼は見事につくりだした。たしかにこれは内側から考えられている。だがこのような自由な床の操作は、鉄筋コンクリートのテクノロジーとの幸福な結びつきなしにはありえない。

The staircase on the 5th level, strangely, looks like a mountain lodge. This might have some connection to the fact that Loos designed a number of second houses. The peaceful and light woody atmosphere is entirely different from the solemn expression of the main hall which is like ancient Rome. Does any other residence have such a variety of expressions? The summer breakfast room has a Japanesque design.[*5] Loos might have been interested in Japanese architecture since he sometimes referred to it. This room, unlike other rooms of the villa, is open to the outside and connected to a terrace. The large hall with a loving height where people gather; the library and the boudoir like a body extension to relax privately; the oriental room connected to the outside, and the light and active children's room. Each room has a suitable scale, texture and color and they form a unified group as a whole. This is the charm of the Villa Muller.

Expensive Material is Unnecessary: toward Architecture like Clothes

As Loos claims in "Principles of Covering," architecture starts with covering the body with textiles that have a soft touch. The ultimate purpose of architecture is to create comfortable spaces. You can consider structural frames to support such spaces later on. The starting point of modern architecture is frame constructions realized with new materials such as steel and concrete. This is obvious in the Domino System suggested by Le Corbusier. Hence, Loos, thinking of architecture from the inside as if it was clothes might look feudalistic.

Let us think, however. Loos created lean and various interior spaces by moving fixed floors freely using the concept of "raumplan." He thought of a suitable height for each room while creating a combination of the rooms and integrating superbly the vertical spaces with flowing circulations. These are, for sure, thought of from the inside. Such a free control of floors, yet, can only be achieved with the technology of reinforced concrete.

Loos says that human bodies are conservative. Architecture can be art only when it is a grave because it does not have a function. Architecture other than that should be conservative since it should follow the physical conditions of human beings. Technology pursues for novelty. There will be a gap between architecture and physical

人間の身体は保守的であるとロースは言う。建築が芸術になりうるのは機能をもたない墓だけであり、それ以外の建築は、人間の身体条件にしばられる保守的なものであるほかないのだ。技術は新しさをもとめる。技術を出発点として新しい建築を構想すれば、かならず身体感覚とのずれをひきおこす。技術はそれ自体が前面に出てくる必要はなく、使えるものはただ使えばよいだけである。技術のために技術があるわけではないからである。

　建築から装飾をはぎとり着衣のように空間を考えることによって、装飾にかわってクローズアップされてくるのが、物質のテクスチャーである。たとえばミュラー邸のメイン・ホールで使われているチポリーノ大理石。その深い緑と褐色のマーブル模様は、人間の職人がつくりあげる装飾的な文様よりもはるかに強く住み手の感覚に働きかける。積層された膨大な時間が内側からあらわれてくるかのようである。

　高価な物質だけがすぐれたテクスチャーをもっているというわけではない。1キログラムの石と同じ重さの金塊をくらべて、どちらが価値があるだろうか。建築家にとってはどちらも同じ価値である。ロースはそう答える。ミケランジェロが手がけた

前室
前室の壁は合板に白のラッカー仕上げ、天井は青の塗装仕上げになっている。日の光の射し込みにくい場所なので、明るい色調の塗装が採用されたのだろう。

Front chamber
The walls are plywood board finished with white lacquer and the ceiling finished with blue painting. These paintworks of light hue were chosen because the sunlight does not sufficiently illumine this space.

メイン・ホール
石が貼られる場所には、それにふさわしく量塊的な下地の表現がほどこされている。ブロックを積み上げたような分厚い壁がつくられ、その上にチポリーノ大理石が貼られている。床はオークフローリング。

Main hall
A massive base expression is adopted with stone used as finishing material. Thick walls, composed of built-up blocks, are finished with cipollino marble. The floor is finished with oak.

senses if we create new architecture with technology as a starting point. Technology should not come first. We can just use whatever the technology we can use. Technology does not exist for the sake of technology.

The texture of material is more focused when decorations are removed from architecture and spaces are thought of as clothes, for example, cipollino marble, used at the main hall of the Villa Muller. Marble patterns of dark green and Mars brown appeal to the senses of residents much more than the decorative patterns created by human craftsman. It is as if imprinted time shines forth from within the marble.

Expensive materials are not the only ones that have a quality texture. Which have more value, 1 kg of stone or the same weight in gold? They have the same value to architects is what Loos answers. They say the walls of cheap stucco done by Michelangelo are shimmering more than the walls of polished pure granite. The value of material itself is different from its commercial value. The material will generate a value when the architects find a suitable use for the material.

The Villa Muller has different colors and materials for each room. The mahogany peaceful plywood is used for the dining room and the library. This texture creates a relaxing atmosphere for dining. The

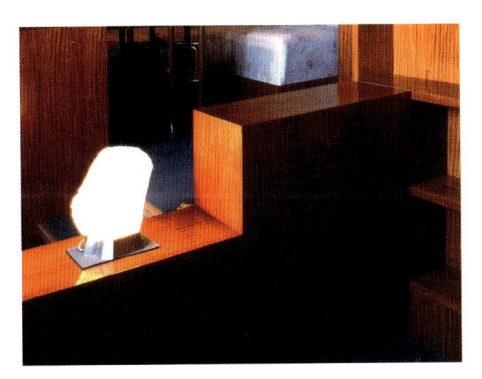

婦人室
婦人室の壁と家具には、明るいレモンウッドの突板が使われている。対する書斎には重厚な色合いのマホガニーの突板が使われている。

Boudoir
The walls and furniture are made of light lemonwood boards, whereas solemn mahogany boards are used for the library.

サマー・ブレックファスト・ルーム
床は紫に着色した蓙を敷き、壁には灰色の和紙貼り、黒と深緑の塗装によって縁取りが施されている。

Summer breakfast room
Purple Matting covers the flooring and gray Japanese paper is attached to the walls. The bordering is composed of a black and deep green coating.

安価なスタッコの壁は、総御影石で磨き上げられた壁よりも光り輝いているという。素材自体の価値は、商業的な価値とはちがう。建築家がその素材にふさわしい使用法を見出したときに、素材の価値が生まれるのである。

　ミュラー邸には、部屋ごとにさまざまな素材が使い分けられている。ダイニング・ルームや書斎には、マホガニーの深く落ち着いた突板が使われている。このテクスチャーによって食事の落ち着いた空気がつくりだされている。しかしそこに通じるキッチンは、一転して白と黄色で塗装されている。近代建築史上、隣り合う部屋がこれほど違う雰囲気をもっている建物がほかにあるだろうか。キッチンは使用人たちが機能的に働くべき場所だから、それにふさわしい明るさになっていて、汚れれば何度でも塗り直すことができる塗装仕上げになっているのだ。しかし使用人たちは、ダイニングに入れば一転して恭しく給仕しなくてはならない。食事の場にふさわしい態度が求められるからである。この二つの部屋を分け隔てる建具の両面には、当然二つのレバーハンドルがついている。どちらのハンドルも全く同じかたちをしている。だが触ってみると、どうだろう。ダイニング側のハンドルは象牙でできている。キッチン側はプラスチックでできているのだ。触感と温度差が、一瞬にしてちがいを伝えてくる。かつて真冬にミュラー邸を訪れた私は、その冷ややかな温度差にどきっとしたものだ。

　子供室は青と黄色の塗装で仕上げられている。子供たちにふさわしい場所として、またおそらく子供の品々がこの部屋を満たしたときに最も調和がとれる色合いを意図しているのではないだろうか。最上階のサマー・ブレックファスト・ルームは緑の塗装に紫の畳風敷物で、日本風の意匠が施されている。寝室には壁紙までが使われている。各部屋ごとに、いかにばらばら

◀ ダイニング・ルームのドアノブ。ダイニング・ルーム側の取手は象牙でつくられているが、使用人が使う裏側のキッチン側の取手は、まったく同じ形でもプラスチック製である。触覚が、部屋の格式を伝達する。

Doorknob of the dining room.
The knob on the dining room side is made of ivory and the side used by servants is made of plastic, although both have the exact same shape. The sense of touch reveals the status of the rooms.

kitchen, next to the dining room, on the contrary, has a white and yellow coating. In the history of modern architecture, can any other example of neighboring rooms with such different atmospheres be found? The kitchen, where servants work, has a suitable brightness and can be painted over again and again. In contrast, the servants should deferentially wait on guests while in the dining room. Proper attitudes are necessary for the dining area. The door between these rooms, of course, has a pair of knobs on each side. They both have exactly the same shape. What will you notice if you touch these knobs? The handle on the dining side is made of ivory and the one on the kitchen side is composed of plastic. The distinctive texture and temperature tell a difference immediately. I was taken aback by the cool temperature difference.

The children's room is painted blue and yellow. These colors might have been purposefully chosen for children and for the time when this room became full of children's commodities. The summer breakfast room on the top floor has a green coating and purple matting like tatami as a Japanesque decoration. In the bedroom, even wallpapers are used. A variety of textures are used for each room. To live, for Loos, is to use the five senses. The houses created by Loos appeal to our senses. Touching the textures, in particular, allows us to fully experience the residence.

ミュラー邸のスケッチ。
Sketches of the Villa Muller.
(Karel Lhota ©)

なテクスチャーが使われているかがわかる。ロースにとって、住むことは五感を働かせることである。ロースの住宅は感覚に訴えかけてくる。とりわけ触ることによって住宅の経験がつくりだされているのである。

想像力はいらない：ファンタジーをこえて

　自由な想像力を羽ばたかせることは悪いこととは思われにくい。しかしロースは、想像力こそ建築家をだめにすると言う。彼は馬具職人の例をとりあげて説明している。あるところに腕のいい馬具職人がいた。彼は、当時一世を風靡しはじめていた分離派の芸術運動の先導者の高名な大学教授のところへいって自分が作った馬具を見てもらった。そこで大学教授は馬具職人に向かって、あなたに足りないのは想像力と新しいアイディアだと断言する。そして自分の学生たちに設計課題をだし、思い思いにアイディアを出させながら教授も自分の案をつくりだして職人に見せ、さらにそれを雑誌に発表するという。それを見ていた職人の目がだんだんと輝いてきて、言う。もし私が乗馬のことや革のことや加工方法について知識をもちあわせていなかったら、私にもあなたたちのような想像力はいくらでも沸いてきますよ。

　ここにはロース一流の皮肉がこめられている。敵対視していたホフマン[※6]たちが装飾的なデザインに走っているのを、ロースが好ましく思っていなかったさまが思い浮かぶ。無駄な装飾を排し、他者としての住み手の生活を受け入れること。想像力を排し、物質の声に耳を傾けること。住み手の身体感覚と建築をつくりだす物質。建築家が徹底的に観察し、耳を傾けるのはこの二つだけで十分である。この両者がどうあるべきかを考えることが、ロースにとっての建築である。物質の特性から導き出されるかたちに眼をつぶり、思い思いにデザインされているものが氾濫している。新しさやファンタジーがもてはやされ、想像力豊かなデザインが面白がられるのは、分離派の時代と現代とでよく似ている気がする。ロースの建築は、現代に差し出された問いとして私たちのまえに立ち現れてきている。

[※6]ヨーゼフ・ホフマン
建築家。オーストリア生まれ。1870年−1956年。ウィーン分離派の中心メンバーの一人。20世紀はじめにウィーン工房を主宰した。代表作はストックレー邸で直線的な装飾を用いたウィーン分離派の特徴があらわれている。ホフマン及びウィーン工房が装飾、家具、食器、庭園までをデザインし、クリムトが食堂の壁画を描いたことでも有名。

[※6]**Josef Hoffmann**
Architect born in Austria. 1870-1956. Hoffmann was one of the main members of the Vienna Secession. He presided over the Wiener Werkstätte at the beginning of the 20th century. His major works include the Stoclet Palace, which features the characteristics of the Vienna Secession; such as rectilinear decorations. This building is known for its ornament design, furniture, table wares and gardens by Hoffmann and the Wiener Werkstätte. It is also renowned for Klimt's wall painting which hangs in the dining room.

Imagination is Unnecessary: beyond Fantasy

Generally, you do not think that a freed imagination would be a bad thing. Loos, however, says that it is imagination that spoils architects. He picked up a harness craftsman as an example. One day, he came up to a famous professor and pioneer of the Secession movement in fashion in order to show the professor the new harness he had made. The professor told him that it was imagination and new ideas that were necessary for the harness craftsman. The professor also suggested that he should give his students an assignment asking for any ideas; to make their own designs to show the craftsman and present the ideas to a magazine. On hearing this, the craftsman's eyes were glowing as if to say, "I'd have a lot of such kind of imagination like yours if I had no knowledge on horse riding, leathers and the processing method of them."

You can find an example of Loos' cynical humor here. It is not difficult to imagine that Loos did not prefer Hoffmann[※6] and others devoting themselves to decoration. He believed in avoiding unnecessary ornamentation in order to express the life style of the residents, and also to avoid imagination in order to listen to the voices of the materials. Architects just have to intensively observe and listen to these two elements; physical senses of the residents and materials composing architecture. For Loos, architecture is to ponder how the both should be. Many were those which did not pay attention to physical properties and were designed freely. What we may enjoy now as in the time of the Secession would be novelty, fantasy and imaginative designs. Loos' architecture emerges as a timeless issue for us.

宮本和義 ©	Photos	©Kazuyoshi Miyamoto Photographer Born in Shanghai in 1941 Since 1964, he has been taking architectural and travel photographs.
写真家。1941年上海生まれ。1964年から建築分野、旅分野で活動。著書に『近代建築再見』（エクスナレッジ）、『和風旅館建築の美』『古寺彩彩』（JTB）『近代建築散歩』（小学館）など多数。		
後藤武 ©	Text	©Takeshi Goto Born in Yokohama in 1965. Takeshi Goto graduated from the master course of the faculty of engineering in the University of Tokyo in 1998. He presides over the Takeshi Goto Architects & Associates. He is a part-time teacher at the faculty of engineering of Yokohama National University, as well as the faculty of engineering and design at Hosei University and the faculty of engineering at Tokyo University of Science.
建築家。1965年 横浜生まれ。1998年 東京大学大学院工学系研究科修士課程終了。後藤武建築設計事務所主宰。横浜国立大学工学部、法政大学デザイン工学部、東京理科大学工学部の非常勤講師。共著に「デザインの生態学」（東京書籍）など多数。		
石原秀一	Chief Editor	Shuichi Ishihara
牧尾晴喜［スタジオOJMM］©	Translation	©Haruki Makio (Studio OJMM)
大石雄一朗	Staff Editor	Yuichiro Oishi
堀井知嗣	Design	Tomotsugu Horii
松尾茂男	Drafting	Shigeo Matsuo
（株）新晃社	Printer	Shinkohsha Co.,Ltd.
アトリエM5 チェコ観光局(東京) Veronika Kristova	Special Thanks	atelier M5 Czech Republic Tourism Board (Tokyo) Veronika Kristova
石原秀一	Phblisher	Shuichi Ishihara

ミュラー邸
1930 チェコ
アドルフ・ロース
2008年9月27日発行
ISBN978-4-902930-20-7 C3352
発行所：バナナブックス ©
〒151-0051東京都渋谷区千駄ヶ谷5-17-15
TEL.03-5367-6838 FAX.03-5367-6835
URL: http://bananabooks.cc/

Villa Müller
1930 Czech
Adolf Loos
27/9/2008 Publishing
ISBN978-4-902930-20-7 C3352
© Banana Books
5-17-15 Sendagaya Shibuya-ku, Tokyo, 151-0051 Japan
Tel.＋81-3-5367-6838 Fax.＋81-3-5367-6835
URL: http://bananabooks.cc/

2008 BananaBooks, Printed in Japan
All rights reserved
Any books with missing and/or misplaced pages will be replaced.